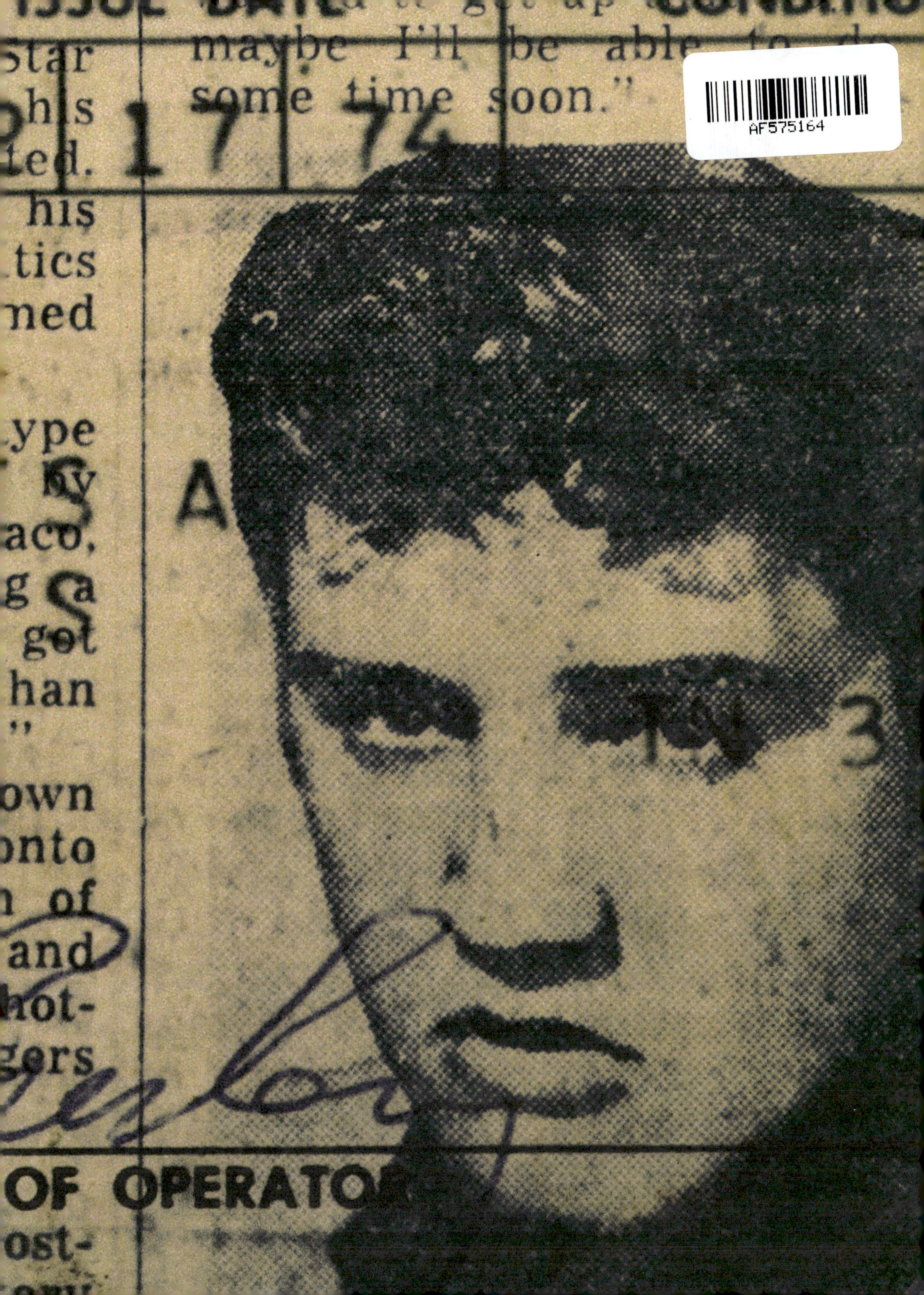

maybe I'll be able to do
some time soon."

2 17 74

star
his
ted.
his
tics
ned

ype
by
aco,
g a
got
han
"

own
onto
n of
and
hot-
gers

A

3

OF OPERATOR

ost-

DATE OF BIRTH

RIGHT THUMB

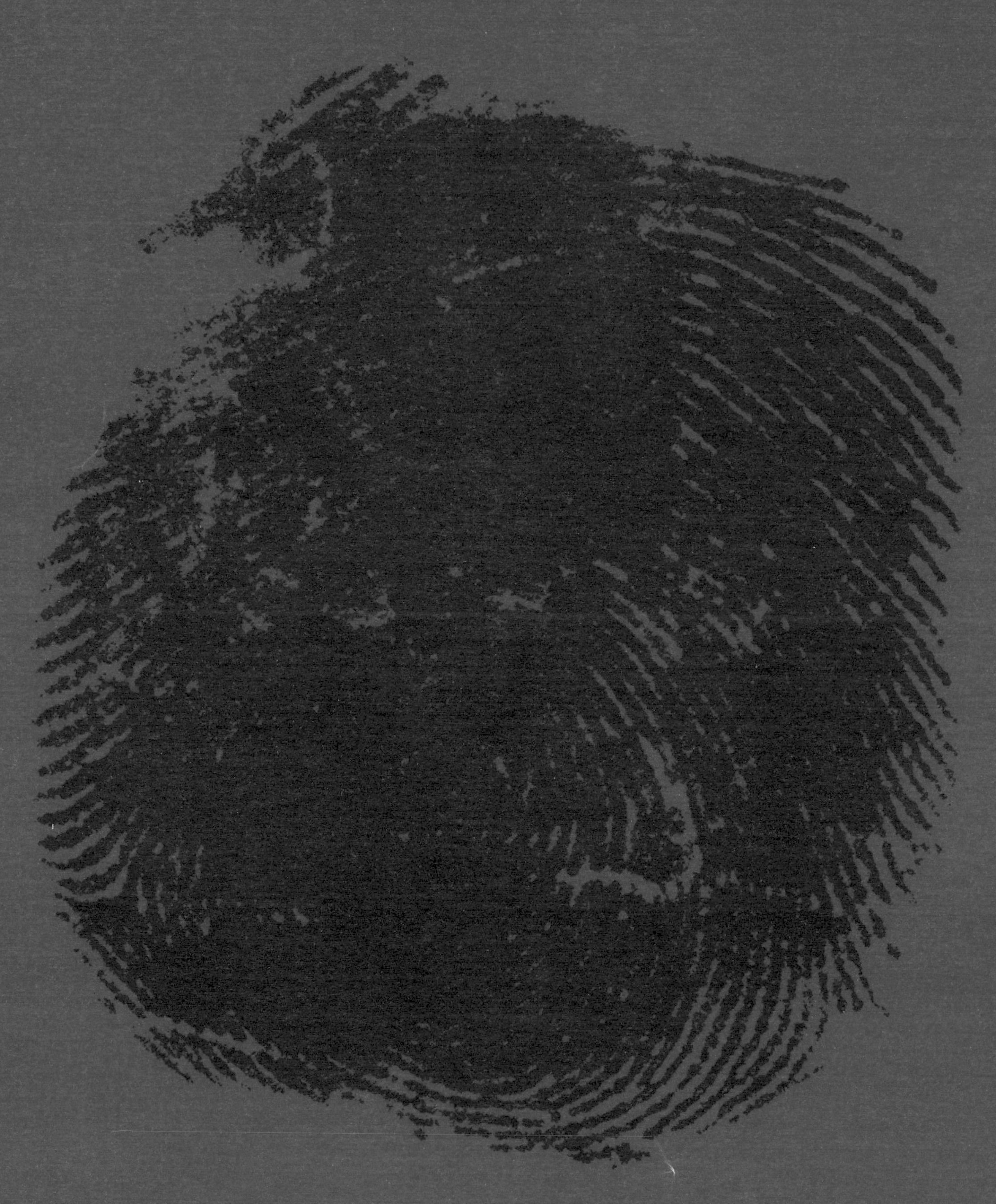

RIGHT THUMB

ELVIS

— The Personal Archives —

ELVIS

— The Personal Archives —

By

JEFF SCOTT

Foreward By

E. A. CARMEAN, JR.

Channel Photographics   New York

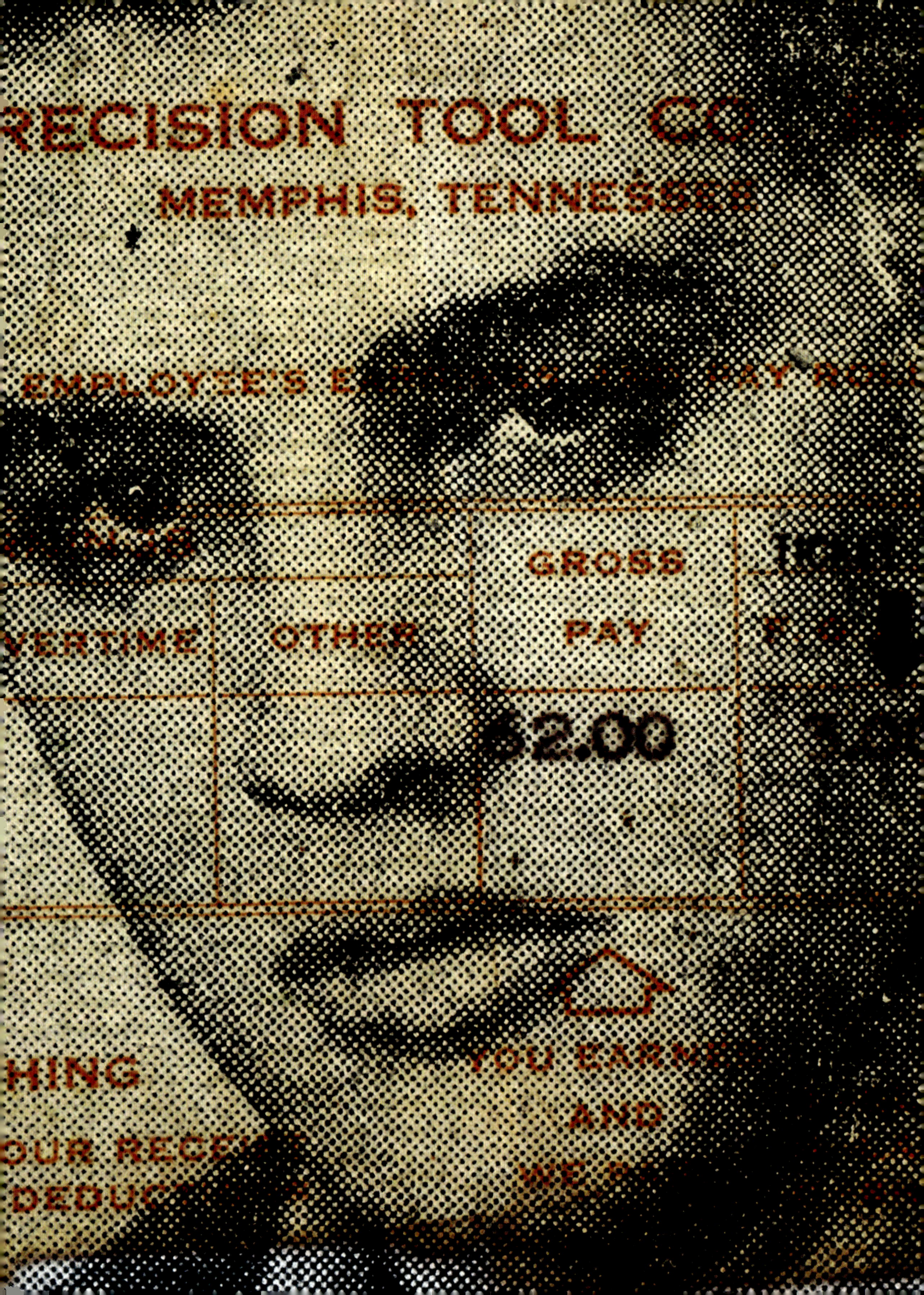

RECISION TOOL CO

MEMPHIS, TENNESSEE

EMPLOYEE'S E PAY RO

		GROSS
VERTIME	OTHER	PAY
		$2.00

HING

OUR RECE

DEDUC

YOU EARN

AND

WE

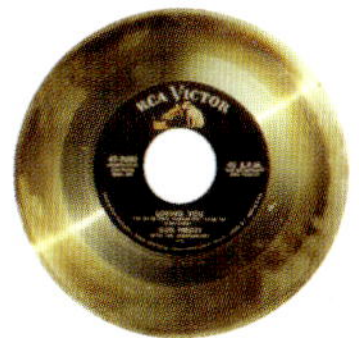

"I endeavor to make the composition tell a story. The chief difficulty I have found has not been the grouping of my [still life] models, but their choice. As a rule, new things do not paint well. I want my models [objects] to have the mellowing effect of age... The rich effect that age and usage gives."

- Painter William Harnett, circa 1890

FINDING A SUBJECT AT GRACELAND

A little more than a decade ago, I accepted an invitation to serve as a judge for the annual Elvis in Art contest, organized for the Graceland complex.[1] While I hold fond recollections of the occasion (including driving through the "music" gates), in the event itself, the artists and their works were not "memorable" — save for one distinctive and common aspect of most of the works.

Although Elvis remains one of the most photographed individuals ever — from concerts and films to life — the contestants' images drew from a limited set of general conventions. Indeed, the works were not unlike those images of Christian saints that employ an established iconography of appearances — a bearded, bald man is likely Saint Paul — and of objects or attributes — an equestrian knight with a lance (and usually a dragon) is surely Saint George. Of course, similar Elvis conventions are used by — indeed make possible — the legions of impersonators of Elvis.[2]

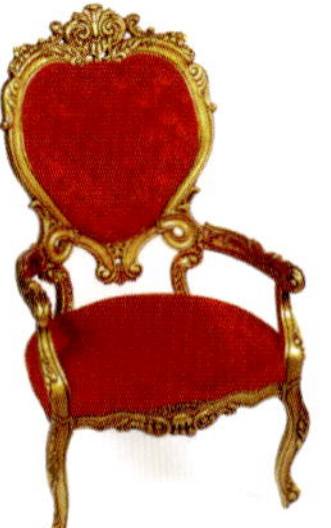

Of course, the Elvis contest entries were by popular — even amateur — artists; and in the world of fine arts, the Elvis imagery used by pop artists depended as well upon this limited-recognizable-range of attributes.

Thus, for myself (and others), some five years later, when I first encountered Jeff Scott's Elvis works at Jay Elkin's gallery in Memphis, his engagement with this subject — in terms of making high art — came as something astonishingly new, being not only unexpected and unusually striking (as captured in this book) but also in holding forth an assured sense of authenticity or genuineness. One might ask "how?" — seeking an answer not by profiling Scott's studio practices, as inventive as they are, but rather in considering the ways in which these Elvis works belong to the modern — and the old American — traditions of the still life.

BIOGRAPHY

One might propose that the modern still life was invented one day in early September 1912 in the south of France, when Georges Braque went into a shop to buy some wood-grain-printed wallpaper to create the first papier collé, or paper collage, of a tabletop still life (actually, Braque had mentally conceived of collage a few days earlier but had waited until his cubist colleague Pablo Picasso — already noted for stealing others' ideas — had departed Sorgues for Paris).[3]

It was axiomatic that the flat, pasted papers employed in collage would introduce a new formal language to modern art. Along with this — and ironically tangent to cubism's abstraction—collage introduced another and often overlooked innovation: the actual or

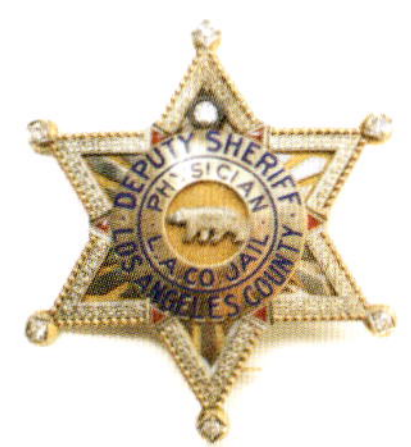

literal realism of certain still life objects effected as Braque and Picasso pasted in real papers from their everyday lives — a "visiting card" left by a friend who found Picasso "not at home," or a cinema program featuring the word cowboy, Braque's humorous reference to Picasso.

Robert Motherwell — who almost single-handedly revived papier collé in the 1940s — observed that his own highly abstract collages of the 1950s were "a modern substitute for still life... a way to work with autobiographical material" and "often... what was at hand in the studio." Thus a pasted matchbook cover might reference meals the artist had hosted at a nearby restaurant.

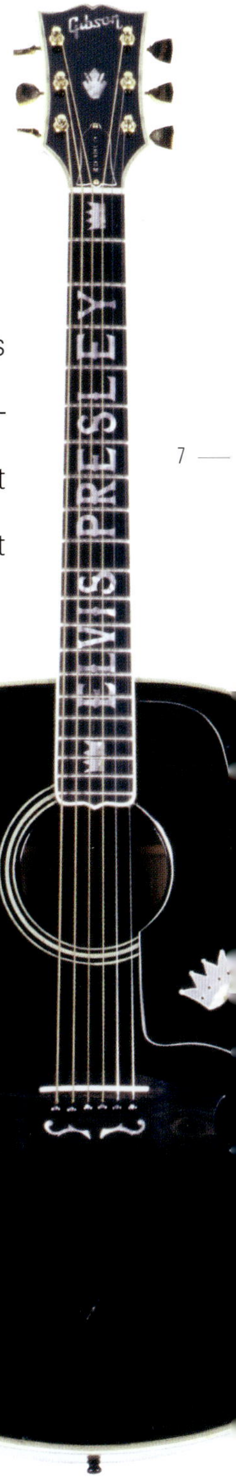

We have looked at this tradition not only because Scott engages collage procedures in these Elvis works, but because it is his insight/recognition that in these "historic" collage autobiographies, it is the "stuff" itself that can tell a story. Indeed, the including of Elvis's biographical elements-images in Scott's work is sometimes accomplished by setting the material (actually photographs of the material) into highly formal compositions; Scott's Birth Certificate's structure parallels a format by Motherwell, and the spare Operator's License accords with compositions by Ellsworth Kelly (see sidebar: "Repertoire").

HARNETT

The combination of objects and words — or more accurately, of objects and objects with words — found in Scott's photographic works not only recalls

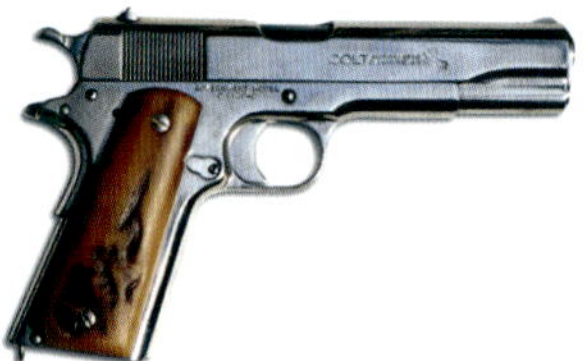

aspects of classic cubist collages and paintings but also forms echoes of similar joinings in earlier American still life painting. Returning to our question of "how?": I would suggest that Scott's works also belong to the tradition of hyperrealism pictures of the late nineteenth century, the trompe l'oeil ("fooling the eye") paintings of William Harnett and others (of note here, in reference to Scott's works, there exists a not-well-known and certainly still-underexplored parallel of "trompe l'oeil" photographs — including "door hanging still lifes" akin to Harnett's — despite the fact that the images are in black, white, and grays).[4]

REPERTOIRE Drawings by the Old Masters are comparatively rare today, in part because their original importance was limited to utility; once a painting was completed, the drawings for it were disposed (one master used his drawings to scrub cooking pots!). Perhaps more than anyone else, Antoine Watteau changed this practice by using his drawings in many works, shifting figures into new groupings (a sort of collage prototype). ||| So here, too, Scott draws from a repertoire of images he created by photographing items in Elvis's personal archives, then using these captured images in a collagelike fashion to form his final composition. ||| These archival elements might also include photographs — as with the image used in the very strong Cinema — as well as actual objects, such as the wooden revolver or the almost iconic gold phone.

The works of Harnett and Peto often portray — in a gathered composition — objects that are similar in a general way to those presented in solo or duo form in Scott's pictures, including guns, musical instruments — Harnett's brass bugle and violin, and Scott's Elvis Guitar — and paper materials with printed or written words — Elvis's permits and license in Scott's pictures, and letters and handbills in Harnett's and Peto's works. Other elements echo thematic functions — albeit altered over time — so that a personal letter in a Harnett finds its communication correlative in Scott's Gold Phone, or Elvis's television set in The Music Room has a correspondent of sorts in the entertainment potential in Harnett's rendered sheet music.

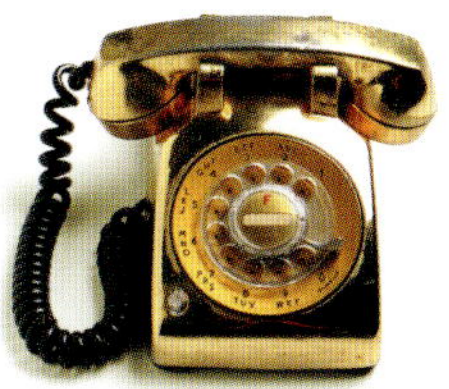

IDENTITY

Scott's access to the personal archives was both unprecedented and uncharted. Thus the selection of the images in these works is his, made to achieve or state a particular point: "The prospect of creating a serious exhibition [or publication] based on the inner-life of Elvis was fascinating to me [as his] personal behavior had not been captured in other art." And to that end, the actual Presley objects provided Scott with a way to "capture who Elvis was as a person," as with "Elvis's" Tennessee driver's license in Identity (ironic title), where the object "reminds us that he was just a guy among us."

Of curiosity, more than a century earlier (see above), Harnett, too, sought to tell a story in his still life gatherings or selections — in line with the broader nineteenth-century idea of "selective imitation," wherein "once selected [for art] nature had to be depicted according to truth."

"MELLOWING EFFECTS"

The virtually deadpan-direct presentation in Scott's still life photographs is in effect a modern version of Harnett's "truthful" depictions. And further — in the formal sense — it allows Scott to create "portraits" free of nostalgia — that "sentimental yearning for the past" to quote the Little Oxford, although here perhaps a more apt definition-meaning comes from the eminent historian of American art, Barbara Novak: "Nostalgia is a way of civilizing the past," one projected by Harnett by his selection of objects already touched by "the mellowing effects of age" (see sidebar: "Elvis").

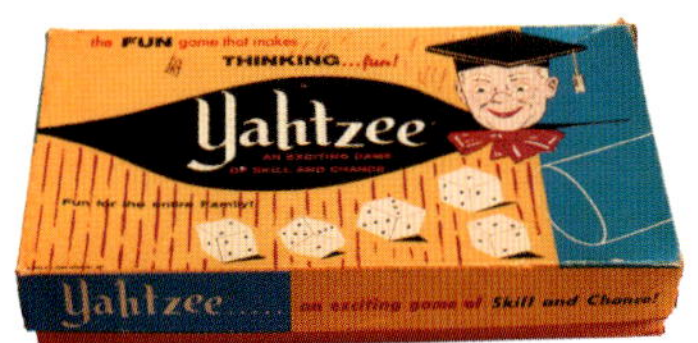

By keeping at a distance a tendency to either sentiment or grandiosity, Scott has the uncanny ability to present Elvis with a deeper — one wants to say (oxymoronically) a "more real" — resonance, while, let us repeat, creating works of art.

Again, as with Harnett and the nineteenth-century American traditions, so too in these photographs we find a point of balance. That is, a pictorial priority is not gained by either the abstraction of the composition or by the "fact" of the presented object — be it an old violin or a rock 'n' roll guitar.

"ELVIS" In a general way, one might say that — contrary to the area of invention (celebrated here) — the approach to images of Elvis is to accept and comment upon common or popular forms of "Elvis." Indeed, for Andy Warhol and other pop artists, their mocking (or dismissive) approach to Elvis's image is dependent upon an established presentation or "brand," as it were (Warhol's Double Elvis is in this sense not different from his Campbell's Soup Can works). And in that odd form of symmetry, so too the fans' adulation of "Elvis" — pace the Elvis in Art contest — rests on the same "brand" images. Just as Saint George has his horse and armor and spear as well as the dragon in medieval images, so too a set of Elvis images is faithfully adhered to by the dedicated.

Contrary to what seems to us to be his ready mastery of rendering still life objects, Harnett wrote that "to find a subject that paints well is not an easy task." So too — if not more so, given an inherent verisimilitude of the camera — is the 'finding task" of the photographer. In Elvis: The Personal Archives, Jeff Scott assuredly finds his subject.

— E. A. Carmean, Jr.

Former curator: Twentieth-century Art at The National Gallery of Art, Washington, DC. Former director: Modern Art Museum of Fort Worth.

1. I agreed to be a judge in part due to a respect for Jack Soden and the reputable manner in which Graceland upheld its high standards in the face of markets wanting something else. Of course, those same benchmarks make Scott's approval by Graceland even more laudatory.

2. Art historian and medievalist Gary Vikan has long studied the relationship between Graceland and relic sites of the Middle Ages.

3. See E. A. Carmean Jr. and Isabelle Monod-Fontaine, George Braque: les papiers collé (Paris: Musee National D'Art Moderne, 1982).

4. See Barbara Novak, American Painting of the Nineteenth Century (New York: Praeger, 1969) and E. A. Carmean Jr., Nature and Focus (Houston: Museum of Fine Arts, 1971).

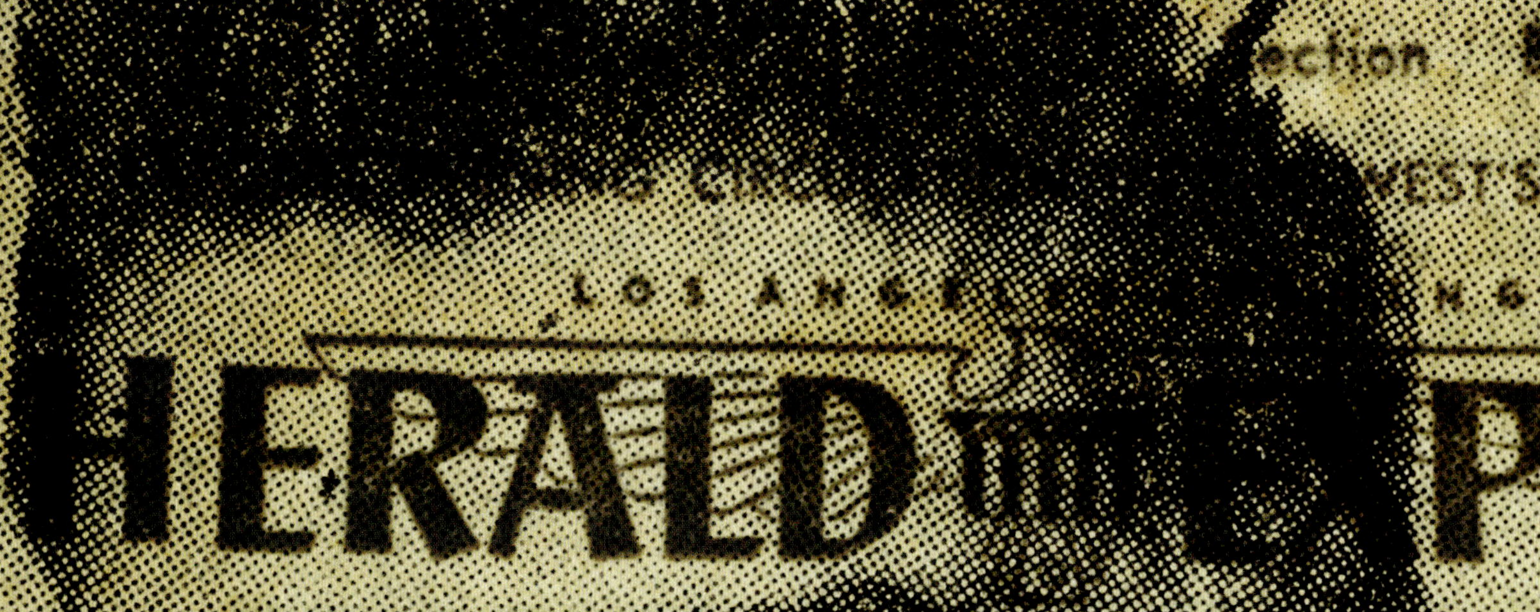

Apollo Resemblance

Like Greek Go

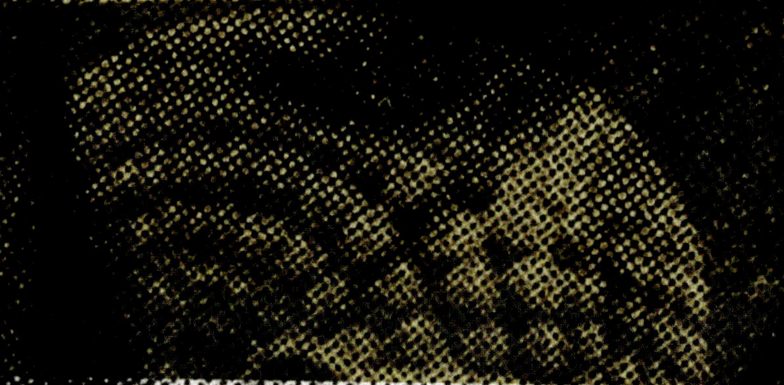

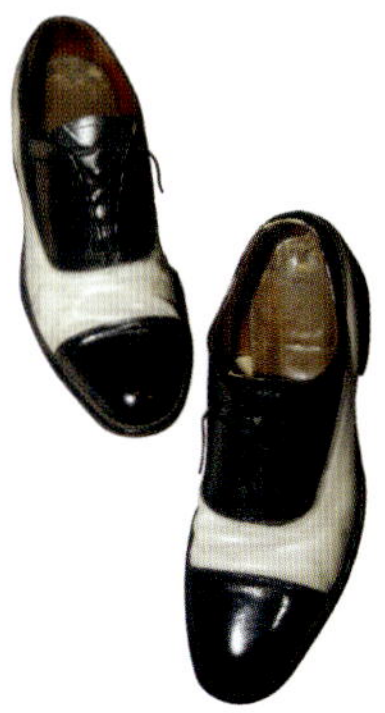

INTRODUCTION

I woke up this morning and a wave of emotion washed over me. It just so happened to be my birthday, and the number — my age on this day — took on special meaning. Today I turned forty-two, the age of Elvis Presley at his death.

It was early 2000 when I contacted the Elvis Presley Estate to begin what can now only be described as a near obsession to demystify the Elvis Presley image. By documenting and interpreting Elvis's numerous personal possessions, I would seek to bring a more intimate side of Elvis's life to the public's attention. My goal was to use the tactile connection of Elvis's personal artifacts and to relate them to our own sense of identity — a subtle way to strip down the image of celebrity and to humanize Elvis.

Over two and one-half decades after his premature death (at age forty-two), the essence of the man seemed to be calling me personally from the grave, begging to be reconsidered by a more complete picture of his life. I have spent the past few years answering Elvis Presley's invitation — via his personal artifacts and possessions — and waiting for an echo from him. The objects he lived with are far from silent. Our personal possessions tell private stories long after we have drawn our last breath. They eulogize us. I am telling the stories of Elvis through the context of contemporary art — as it is my desire to make his individuality visceral once again — but this time through the power of his most private possessions.

These photographic works began with an assumption punctuated by questions about what Elvis was really like, behind closed doors. I used images of his objects as

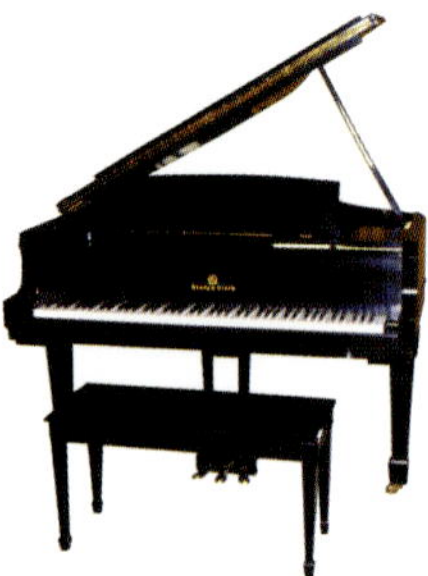

physical evidence of an ordinary man, with the goal of producing a new relationship between Elvis and his public. These items provided me with mounds of subtext, containing many enigmatic clues to his personality. For example, in the work *Object of Authority*, I paired the narcotics badge given to Elvis by President Nixon in 1970 with one of Elvis's favorite pistols, providing the viewer with a look at the paradox of Elvis's rebellious reputation and his lifelong obsession with authoritative symbols.

However, attaching meaning to trivia, I have since learned, is a subjective business, since objects are experienced, and the experiences are not entirely replicable. The success of my mission to reconnect with a more personal Elvis felt like a large challenge, both then and now. I would find out soon enough that deconstructing celebrity culture is a tricky business. The images of Elvis kept coming back to me and affected my personal view of his objects. The more I wished to find the common man, the more I became stuck in the novelty of who I was really dealing with.

His Tennessee driver's license, as I handled it, was frayed and worn and felt much like my own. Turning it over in my hands, it revealed its connection with his own humanity, its identification number a humble reminder that he was just a man among us. In *Gold Bedside Telephone*, this was not just a simple artifact of the larger-than-life communicator on stage — widely known to the world — but a far more intimate symbol. This object represented to me a symbol of the quiet side of the man, hanging back in his own isolated domain, far away from prying eyes and the desires of others.

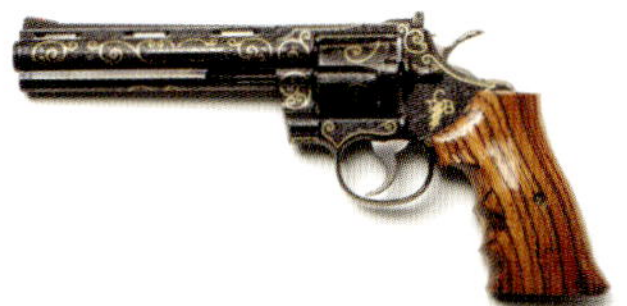

The challenge of this project was to keep the objects interesting without succumbing to the temptation to use Elvis's image superfluously. After all, from infancy, it is the human face that soothes and centers us. But in the spirit of renewal and with the clear objective of meeting Elvis on human terms — his terms — I wish to invite the reader to meet up with him once again and look out into the world through his eyes, not just into them.

— Jeff Scott

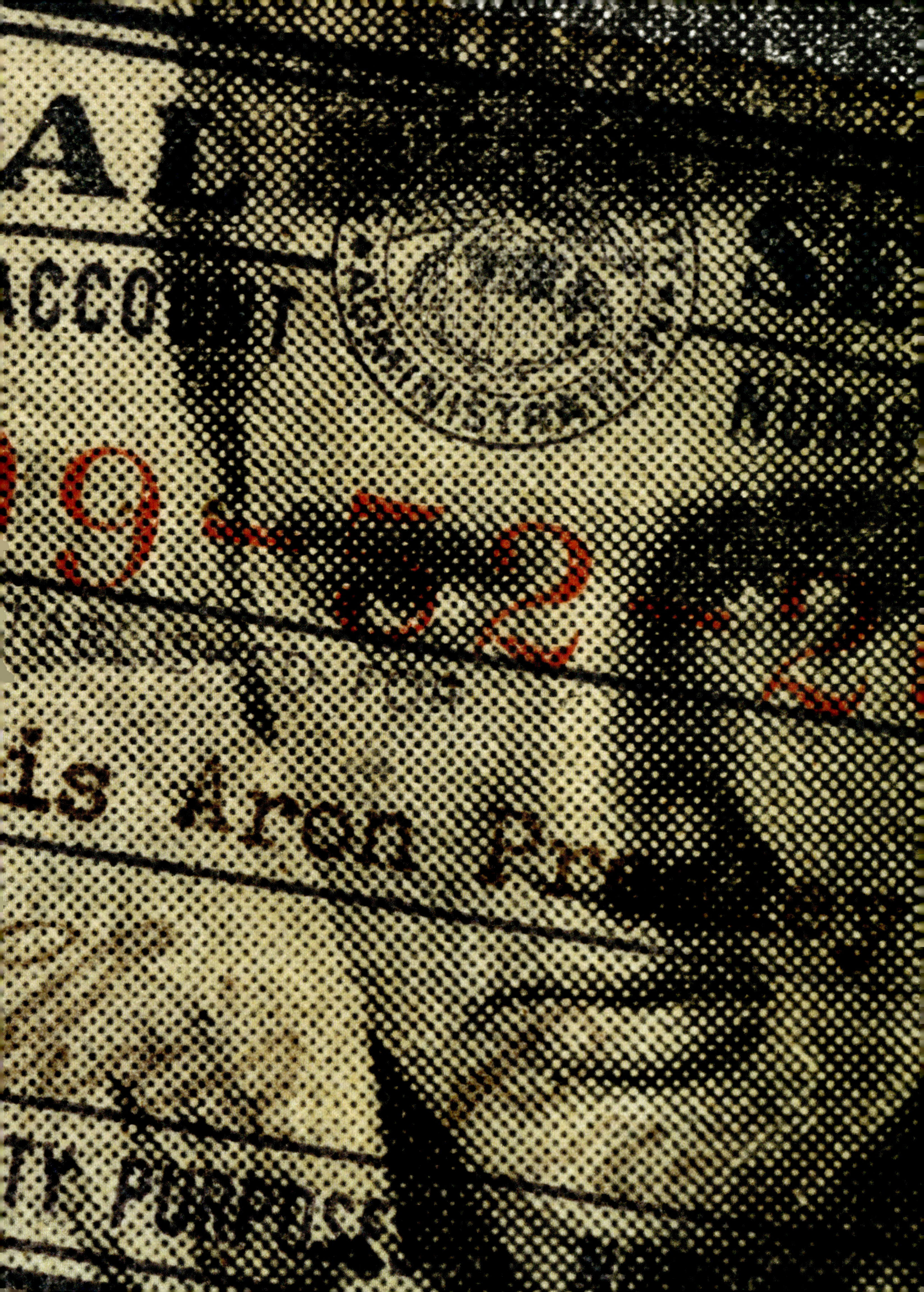
ACCO
9-52-2
is Aren Fr
PURPOS

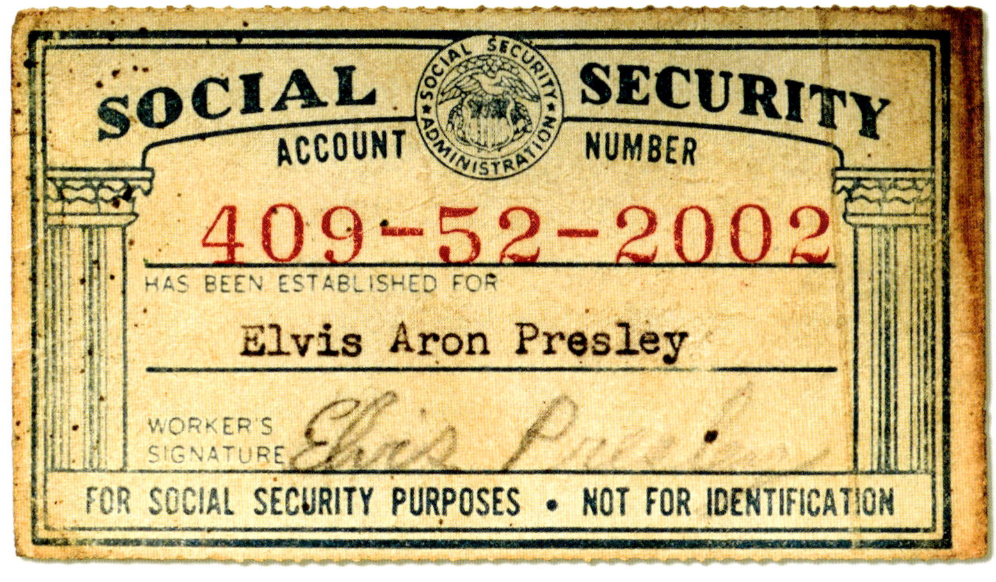
SOCIAL SECURITY
ACCOUNT NUMBER
SOCIAL SECURITY ADMINISTRATION
409-52-2002
HAS BEEN ESTABLISHED FOR
Elvis Aron Presley
WORKER'S SIGNATURE
FOR SOCIAL SECURITY PURPOSES • NOT FOR IDENTIFICATION

Gold Bedside Telephone
Elvis held intimate conversations from the privacy of his bedroom on this bedside phone.

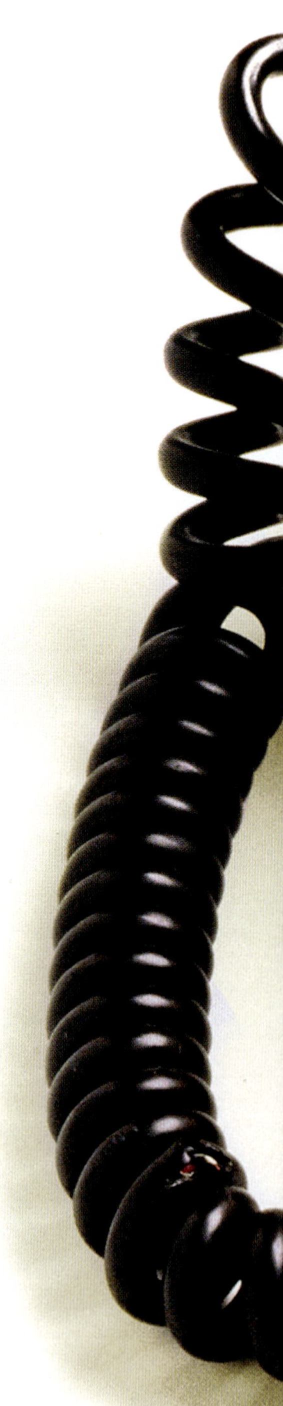

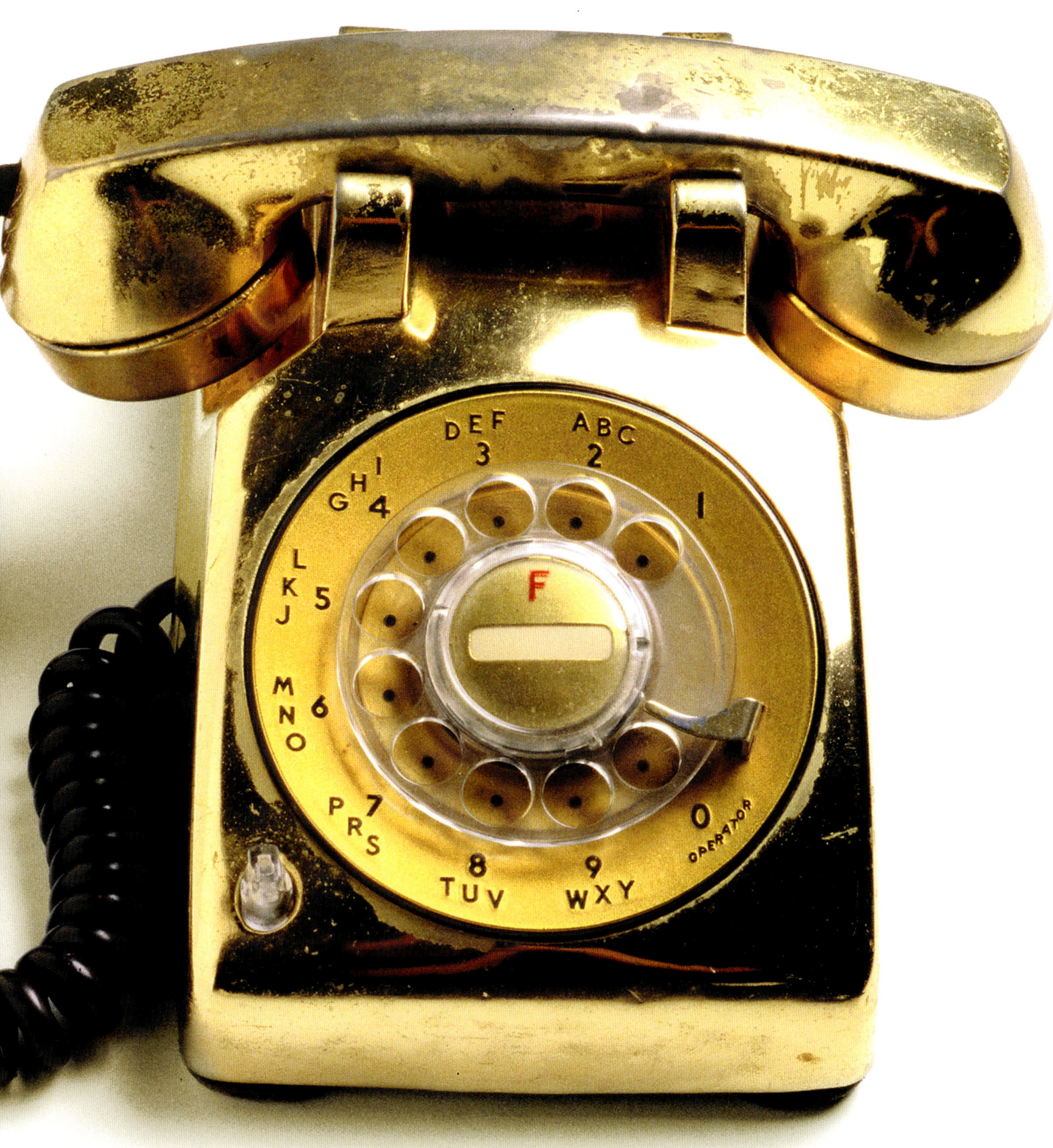
DEF
3
ABC
2
1
GHI
4
JKL
5
F
MNO
6
PRS
7
8
TUV
9
WXY
0
OPERATOR

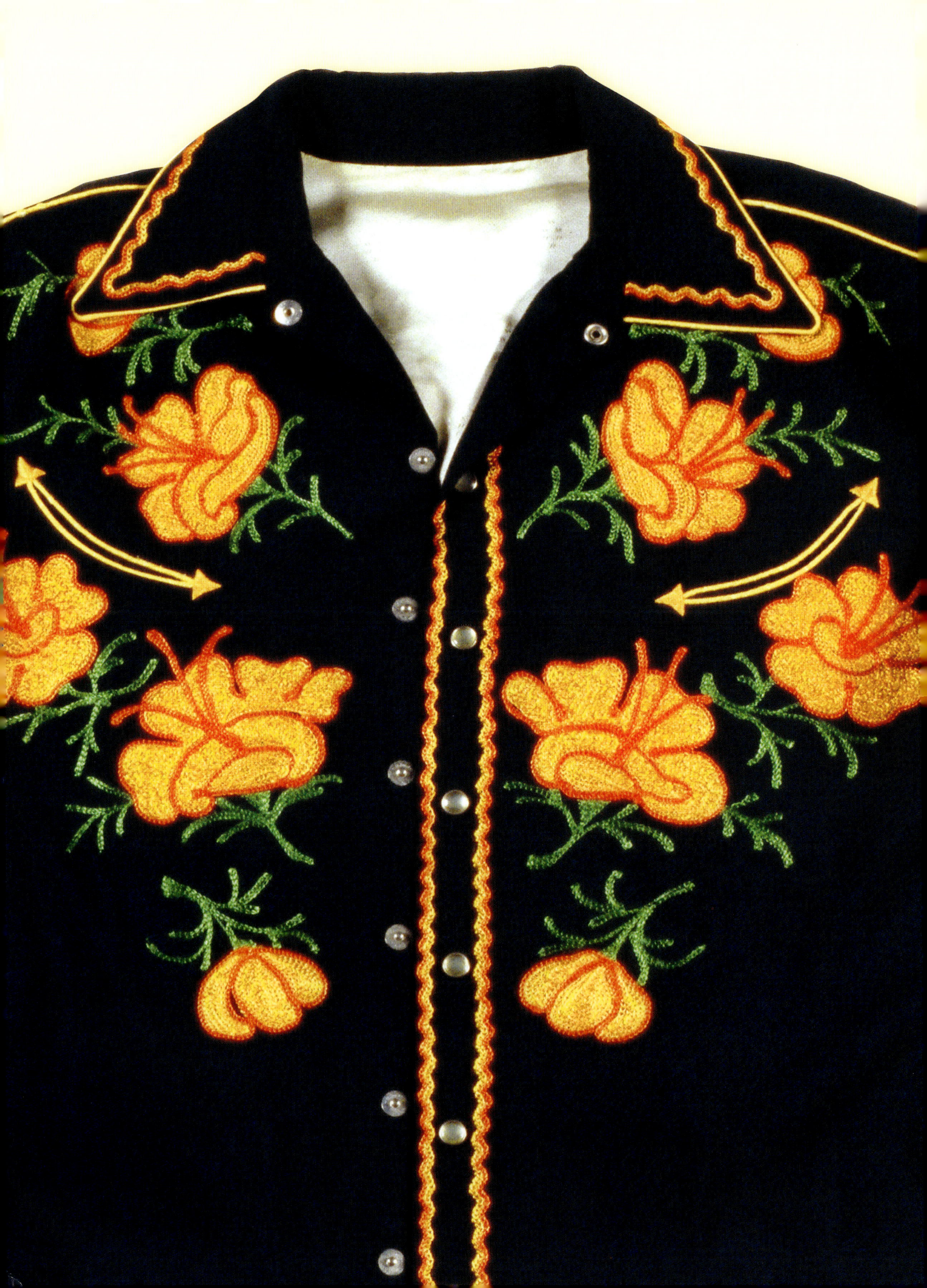

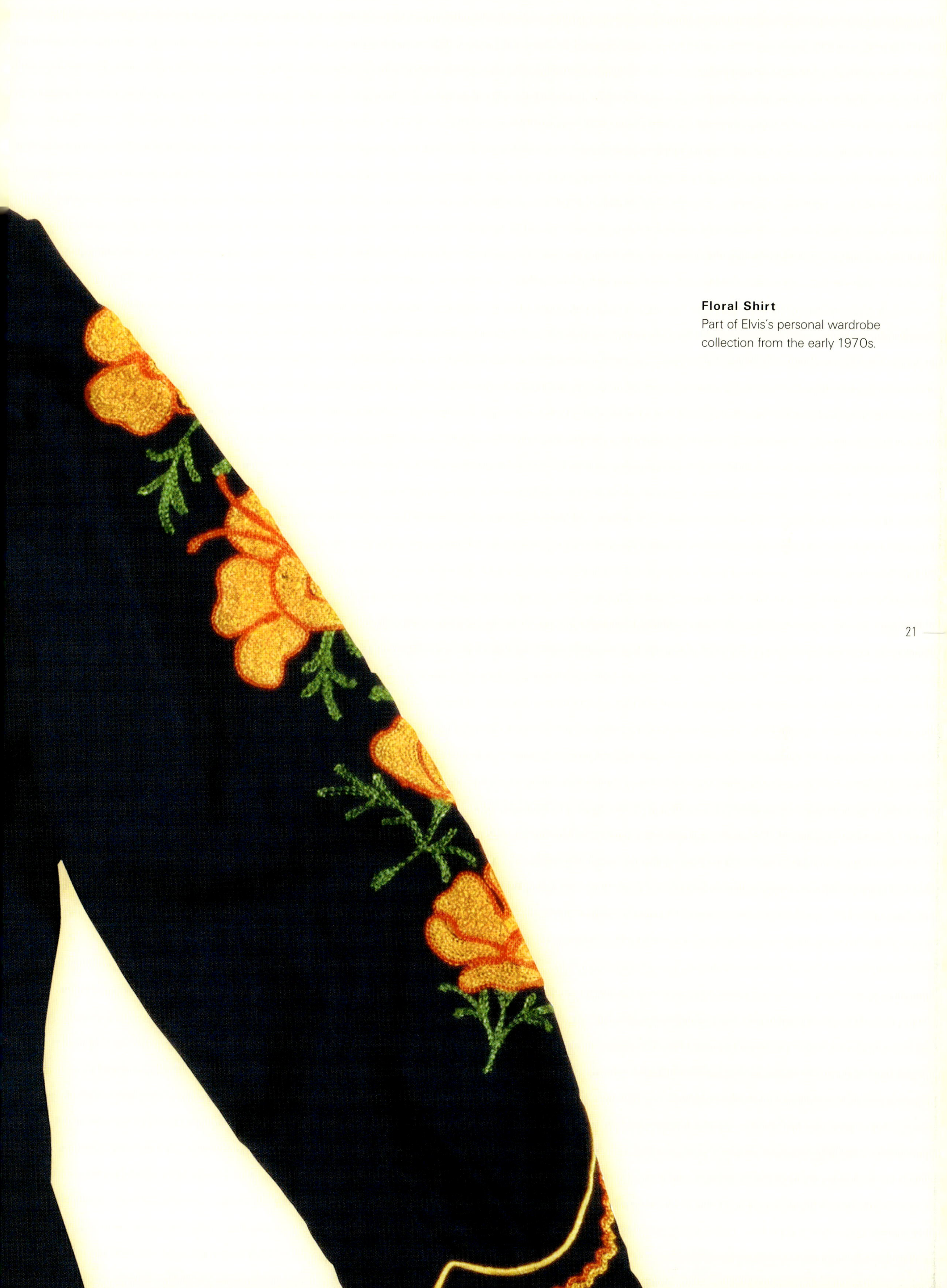

Floral Shirt
Part of Elvis's personal wardrobe collection from the early 1970s.

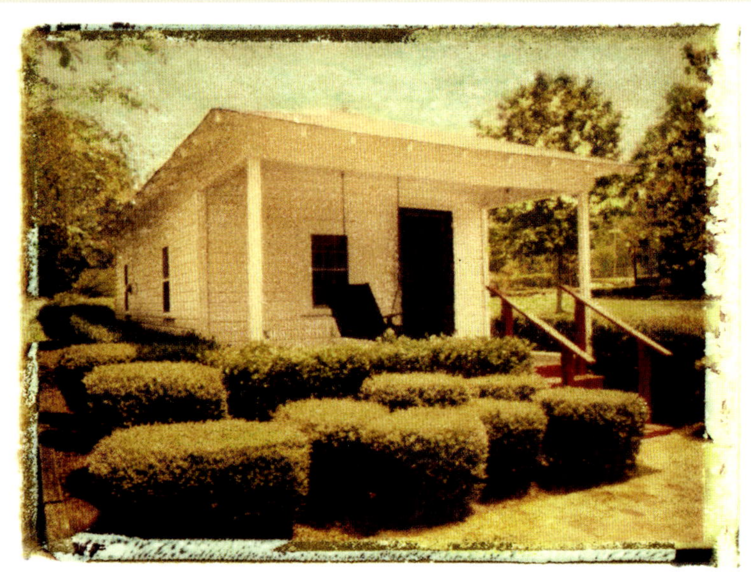

Tupelo Birth Home
Elvis's birthplace in Tupelo, Mississippi.

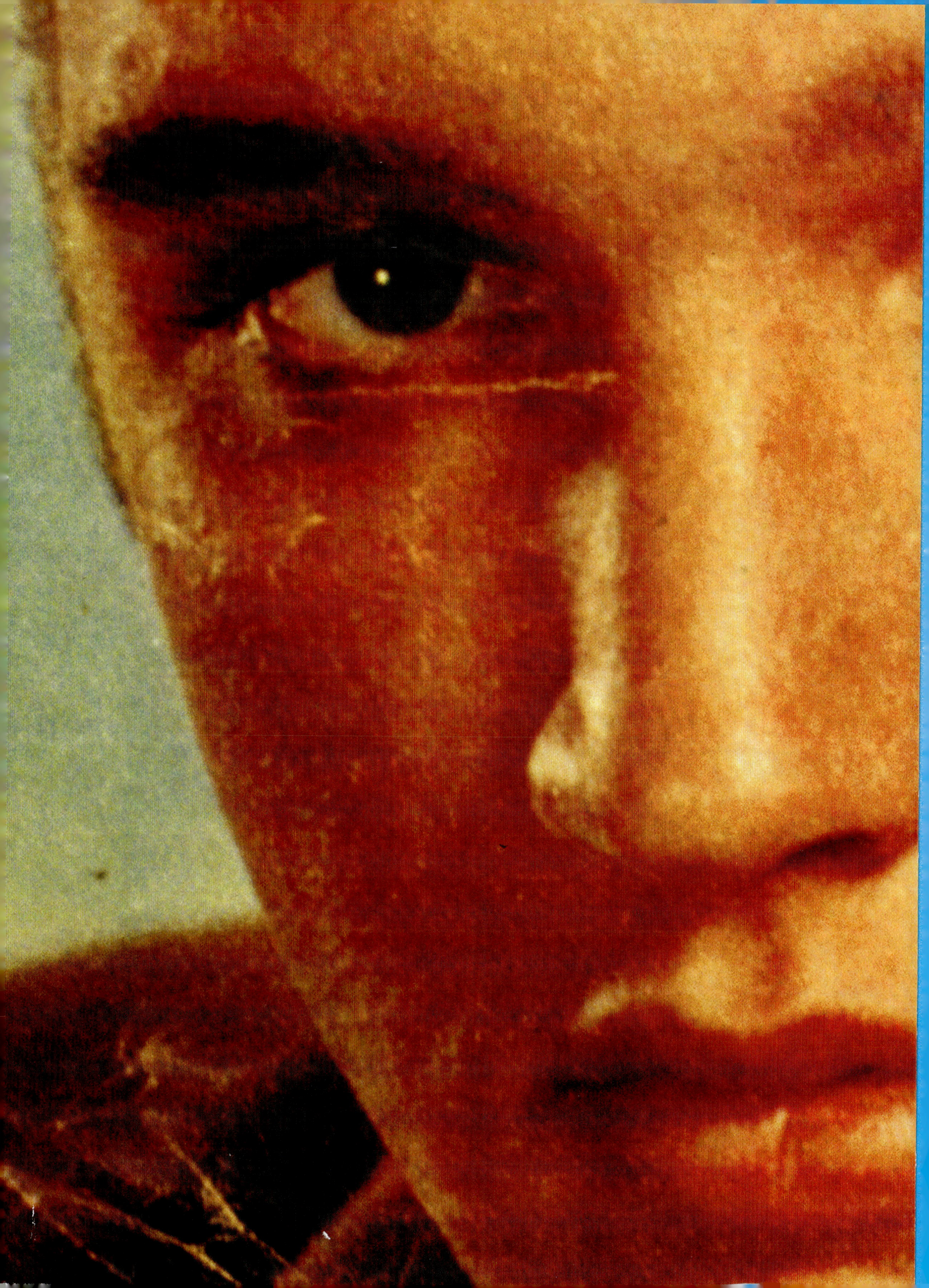

Colt 45

This turquoise engraved Colt .45 semi-automatic was one of Elvis's favorite pistols and has his initials inlaid on the handle of the gun.

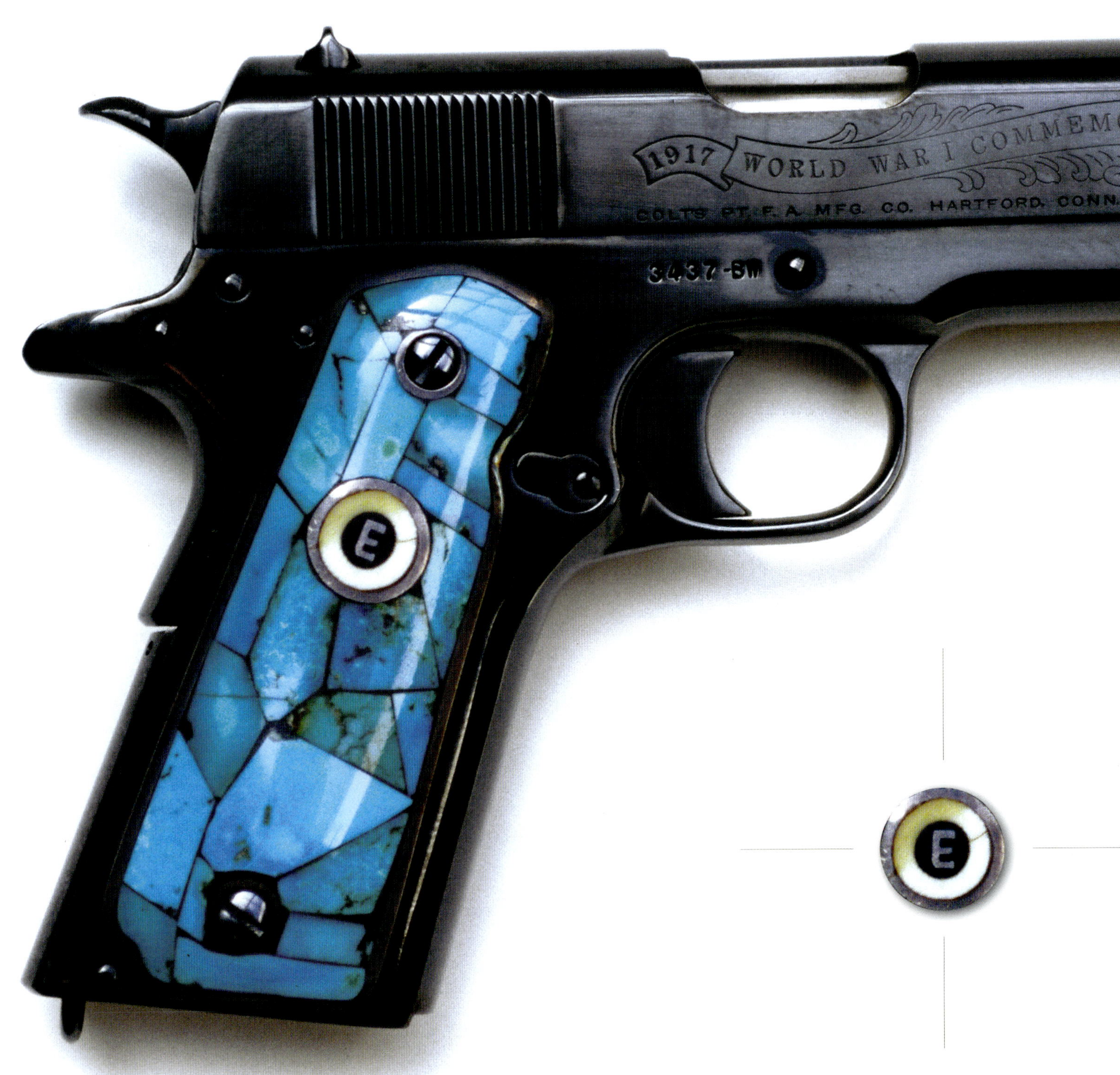

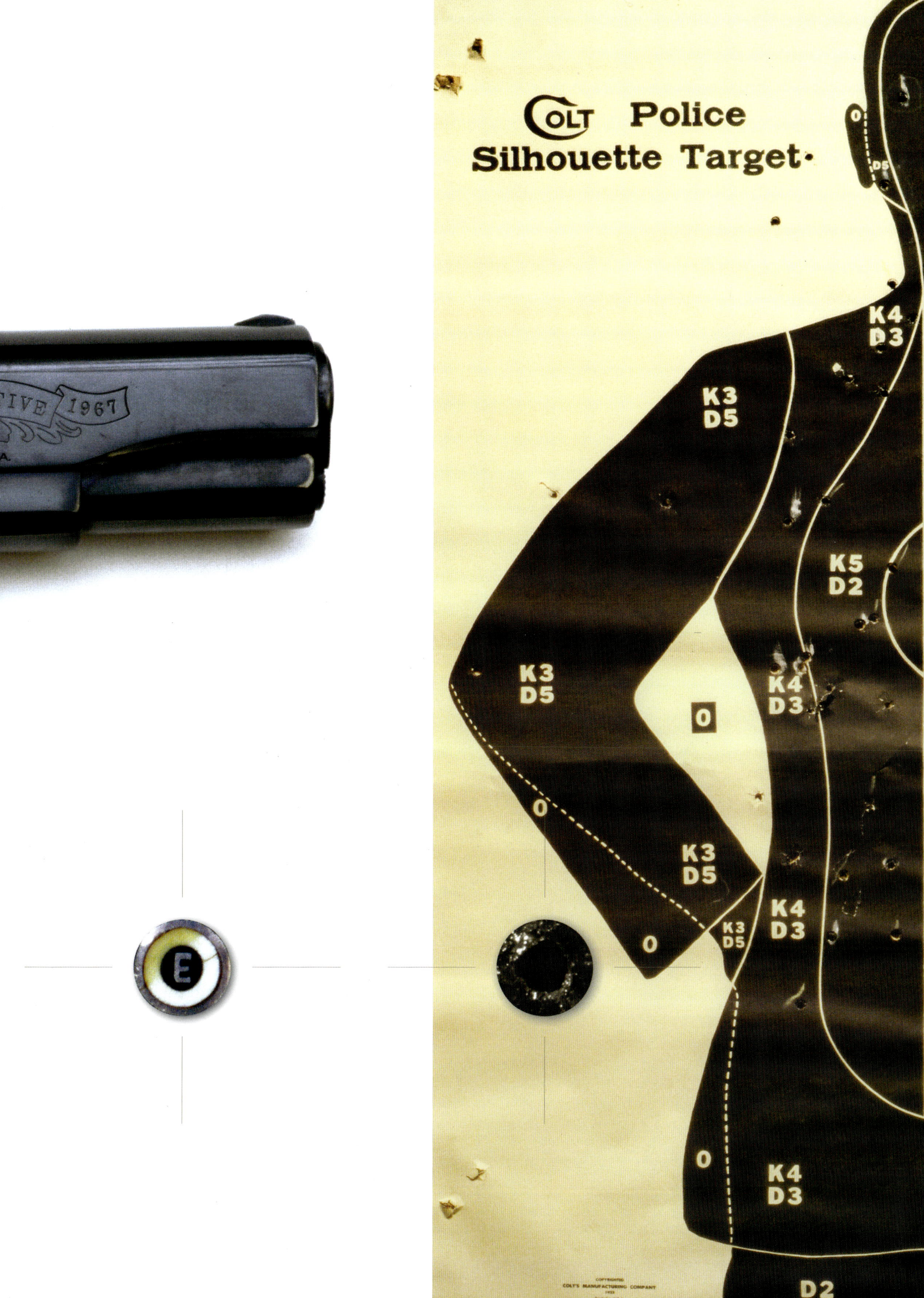
TIVE 1967
COLT Police
Silhouette Target
K4
D3
K3
D5
K5
D2
K3
D5
O
K4
D3
O
K3
D5
K3
D5
K4
D3
O
O
K4
D3
D2
E

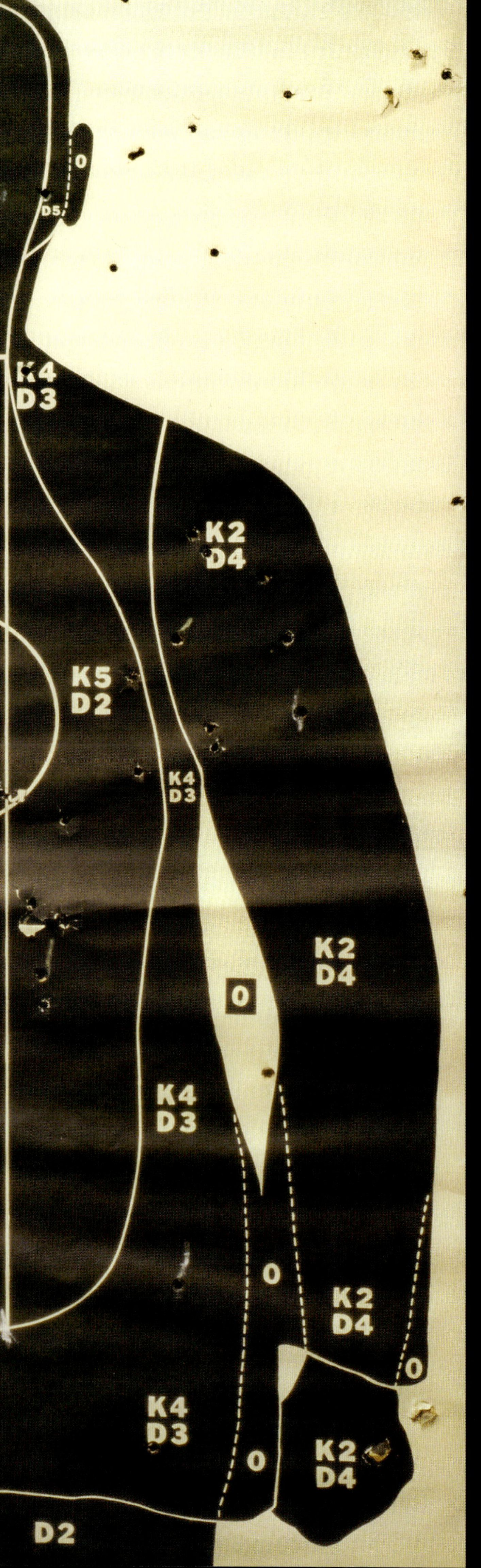

Target
Elvis and his Memphis Mafia would shoot out targets in his backyard after returning from a long tour.

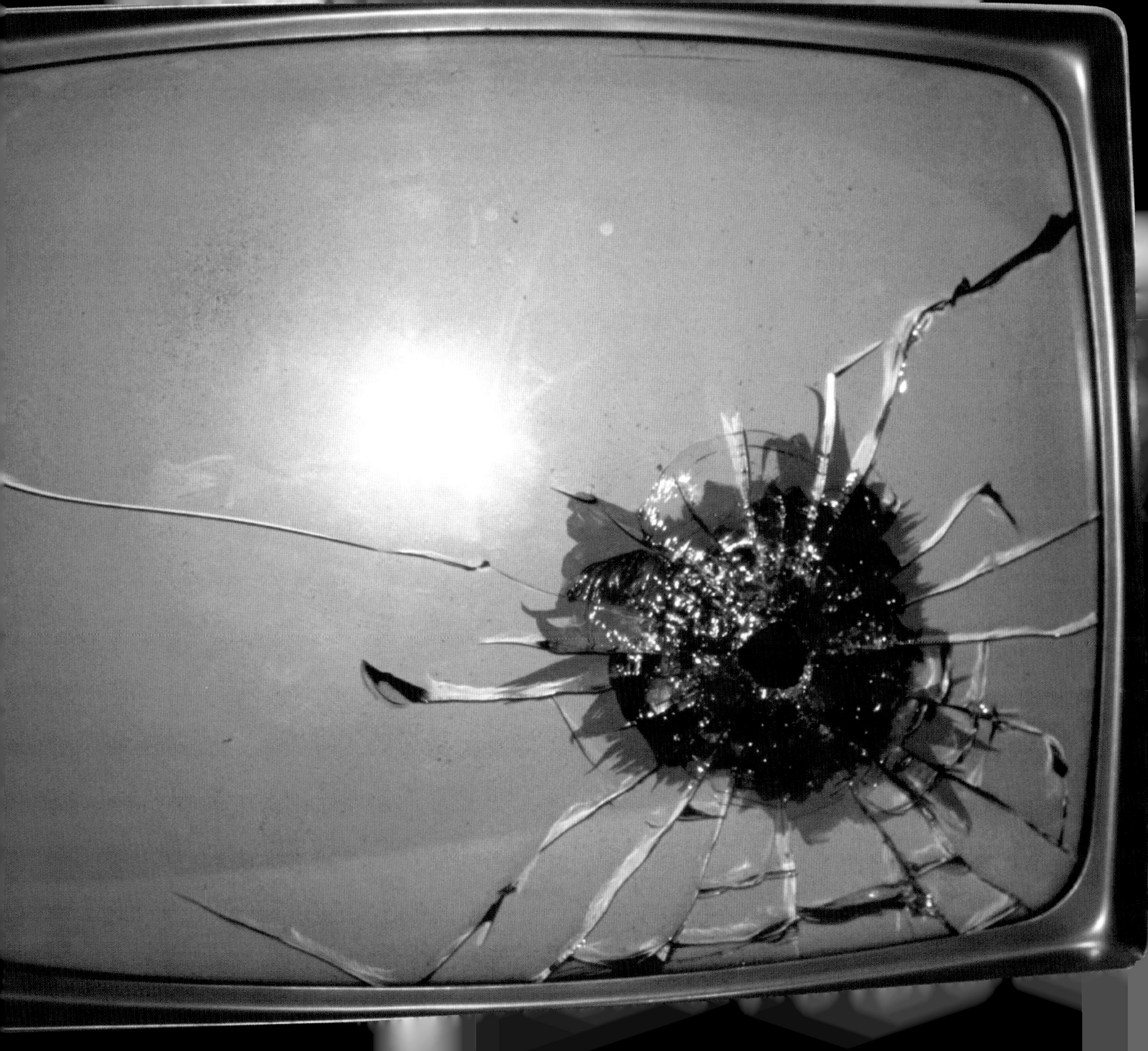

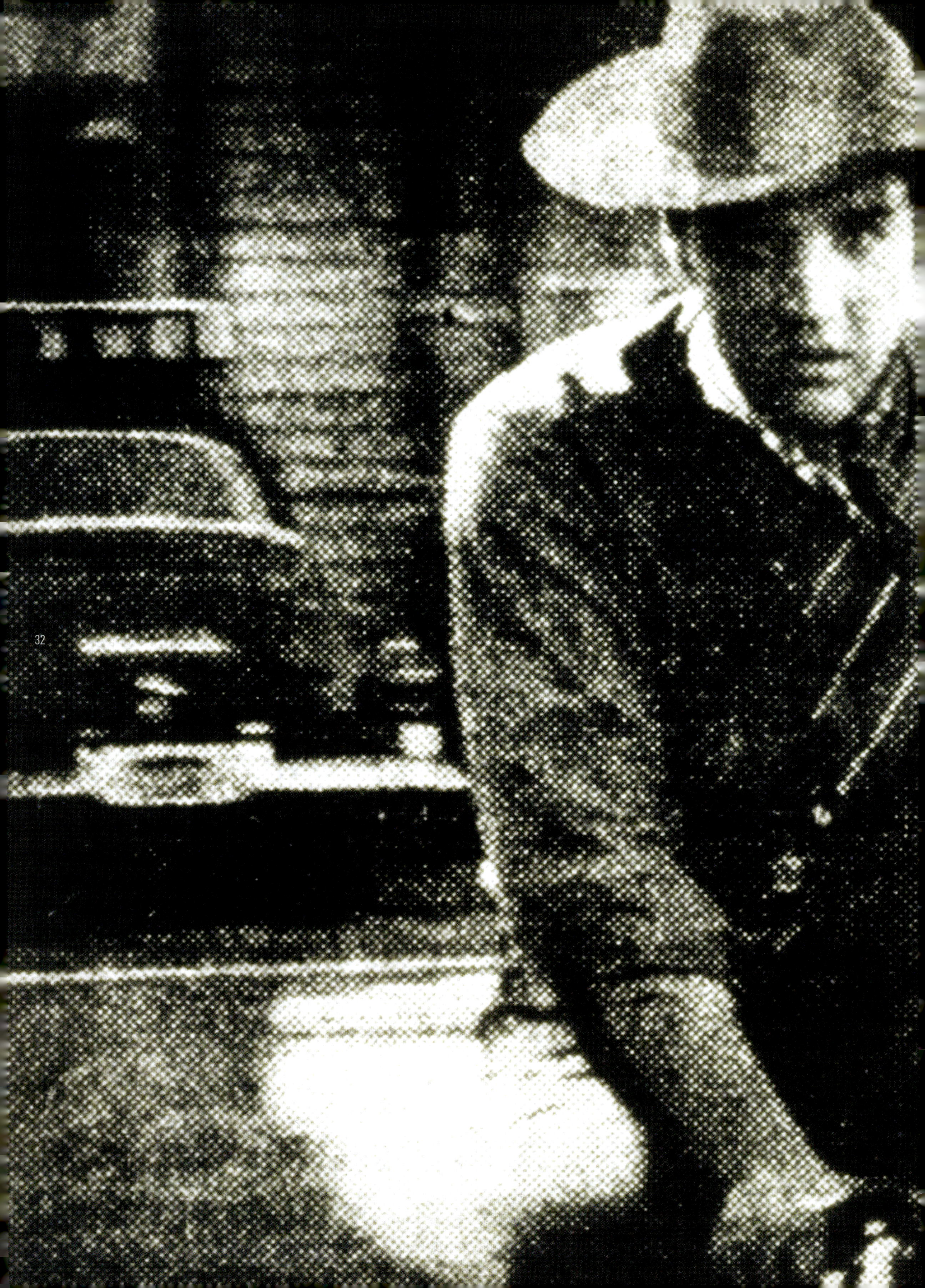

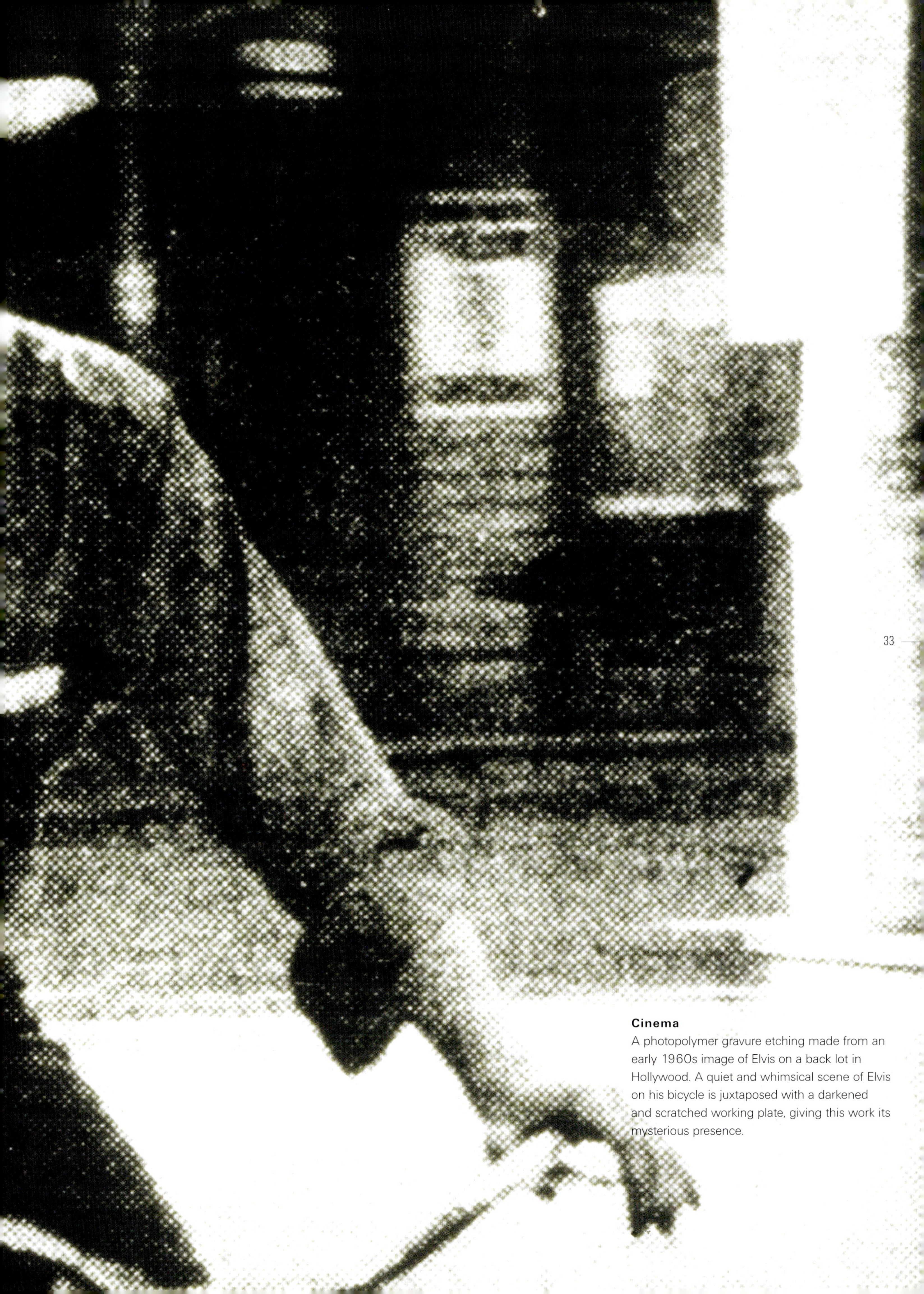

Cinema

A photopolymer gravure etching made from an early 1960s image of Elvis on a back lot in Hollywood. A quiet and whimsical scene of Elvis on his bicycle is juxtaposed with a darkened and scratched working plate, giving this work its mysterious presence.

Music Room TV
Elvis used this 1950s-era RCA TV with family and friends. Bought before his move to Graceland, it was a nostalgic reminder of his early years.

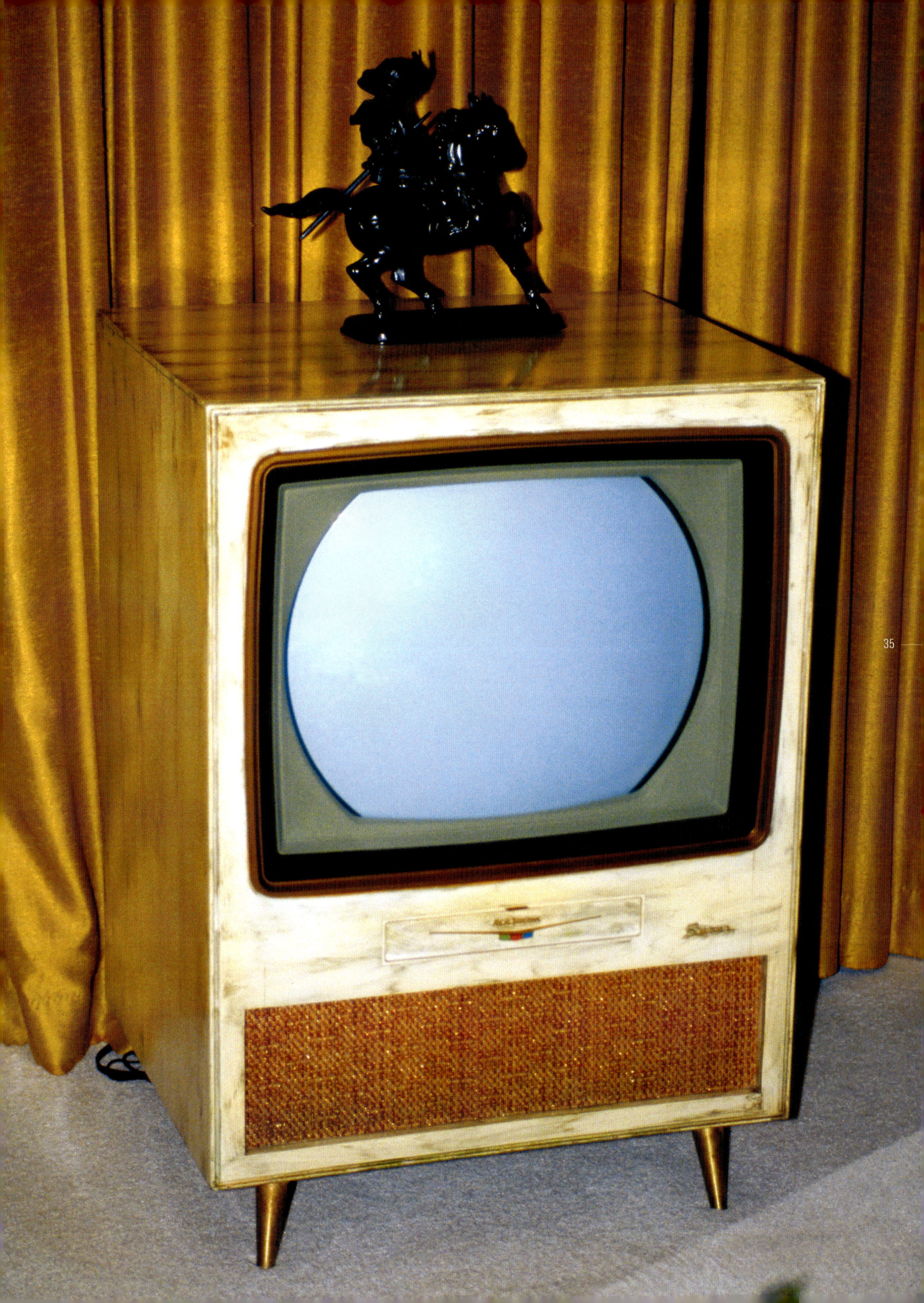

Guitar
Elvis's favorite guitar, a 1956 Gibson J-200. The pearl inlay in the neck and the custom pick guard were added when Elvis had Scotty send this guitar to Gibson to have it refurbished in March 1960.

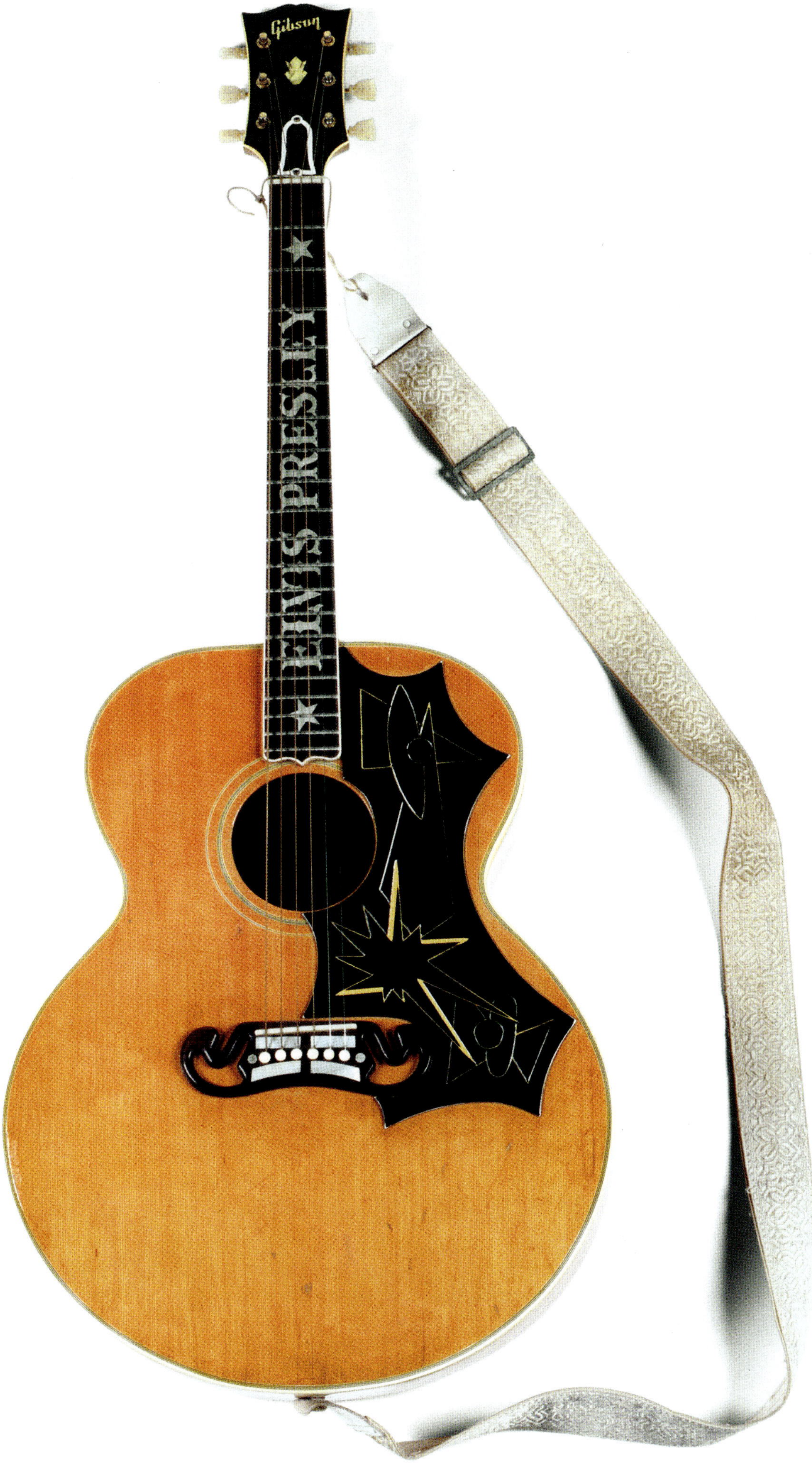

Visionary
This photopolymer gravure etching shows an elusive Elvis hanging out on a film set in the 1960's.

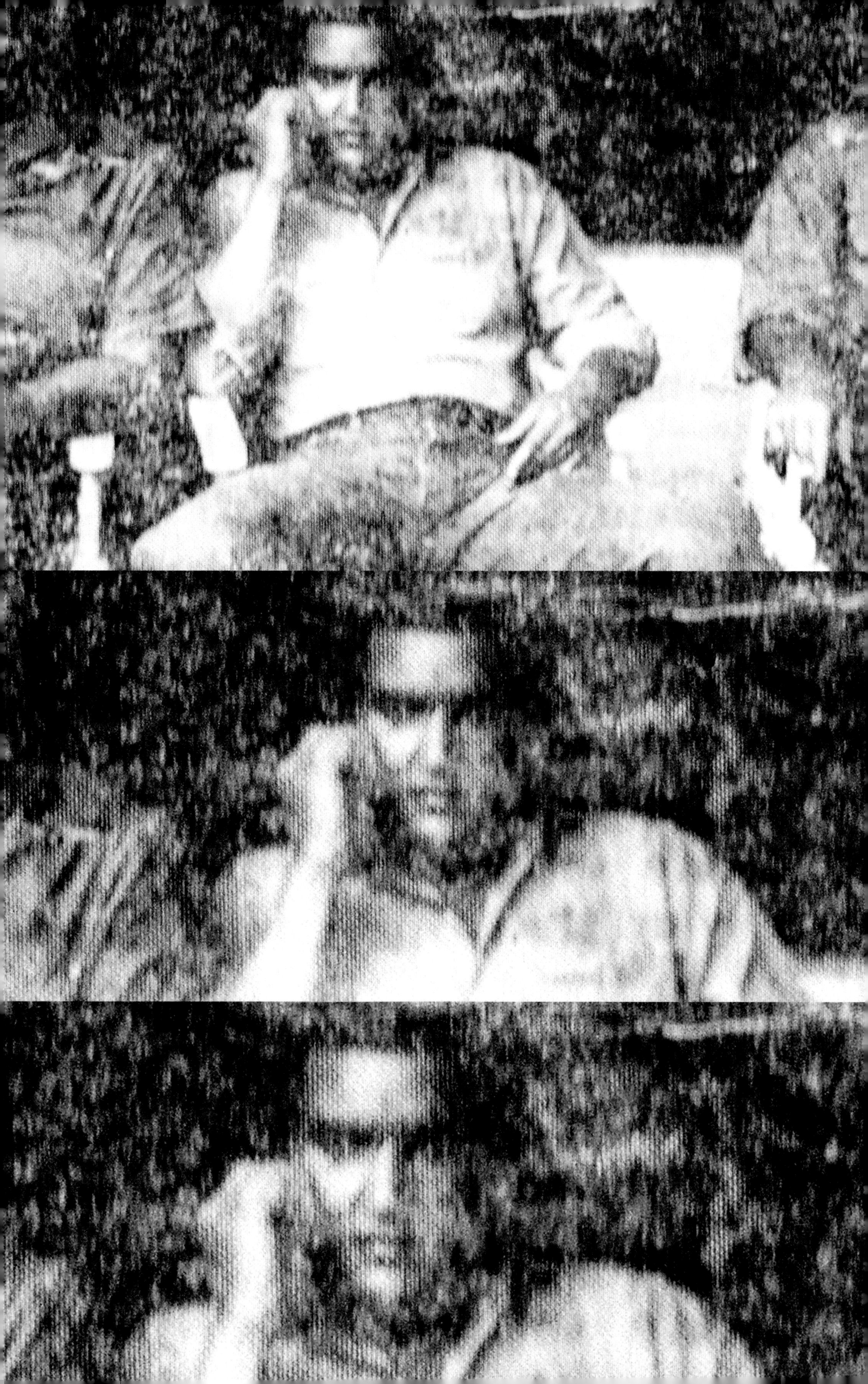

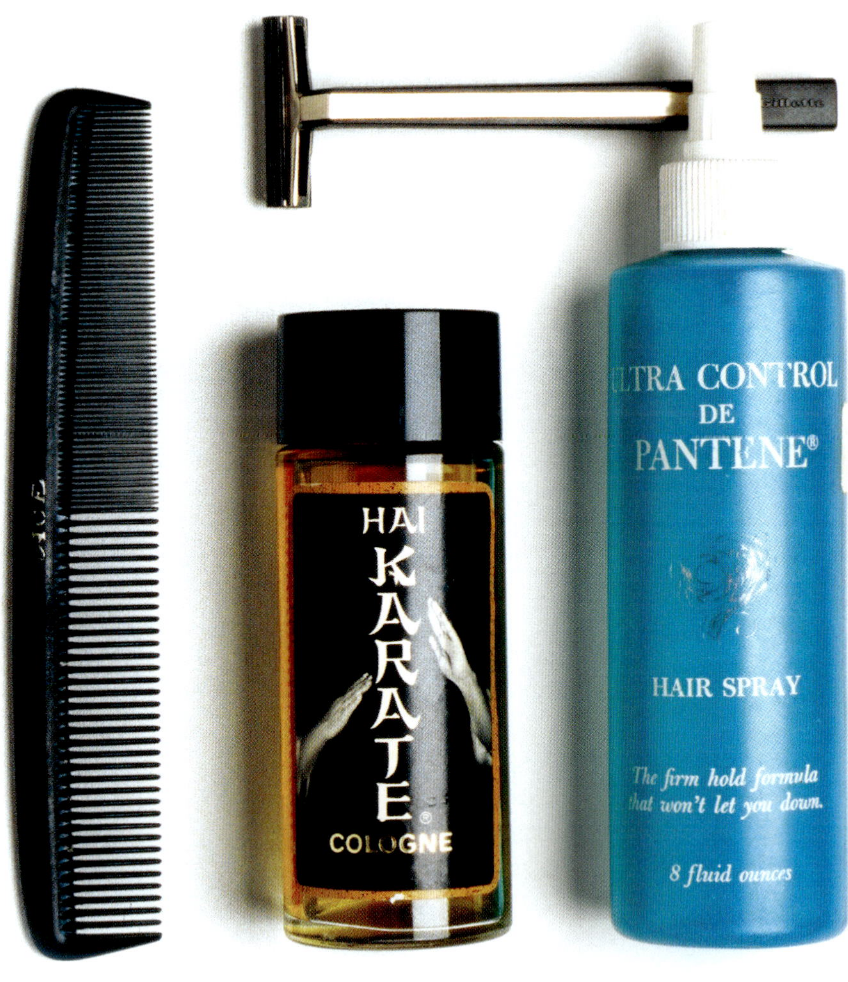
HAI
KARATE
COLOGNE
ULTRA CONTROL
DE
PANTENE®
HAIR SPRAY
The firm hold formula
that won't let you down.
8 fluid ounces

Hai Karate Still Life
Artifacts taken from Elvis's medicine cabinet.

Clipped
A photopolymer gravure image of Elvis getting his hair cut for the army in 1958. This photograph was taken at Fort Chaffee, Arkansas.

Army Card
One of several pieces of army identification that Elvis needed in the service. This one was his driver's license, allowing him to drive tanks and military jeeps.

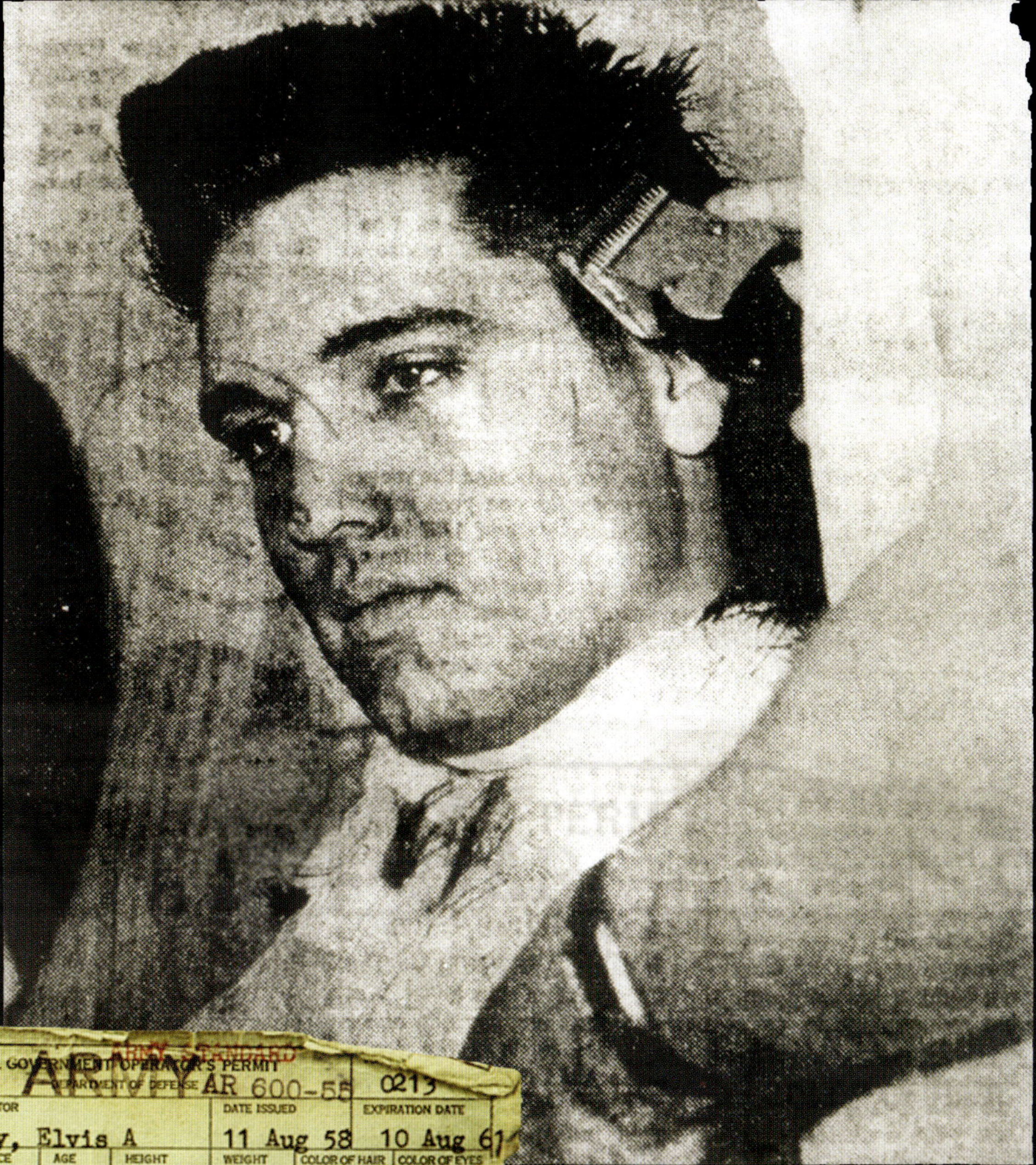

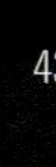

US ARMY — ARMY STANDARD
U. S. GOVERNMENT OPERATOR'S PERMIT
DEPARTMENT OF DEFENSE AR 600-55 0213

NAME OF OPERATOR				DATE ISSUED		EXPIRATION DATE
Presley, Elvis A				11 Aug 58		10 Aug 61
SEX	RACE	AGE	HEIGHT	WEIGHT	COLOR OF HAIR	COLOR OF EYES
Male	Cau	23	6'	180	Brown	Blue

The holder of this permit is qualified to operate U. S. Government vehicles and/or equipment specified subject to the restrictions set forth on the reverse hereof.

SIGNATURE OF ISSUING OFFICIAL — TITLE CWO-3 USA

NAME AND LOCATION OF ISSUING UNIT Hq 2d Med Tk Bn (Patton) 37th Armor, 2d AD, Fort Hood, Texas

NOT TRANSFERABLE *Permit must be carried at all times when operating Government vehicles.*

SIGNATURE OF OPERATOR (Not valid unsigned)

D FORM 313, 1 AUG 50 REPLACES WD AGO FORM 9-74, 1 AUG 48, WHICH MAY BE USED.

THE TAM

TIONS — 162 PAGES TAMPA, FLORI

GOT UP AT 3 A.M.—

Only 2 Girls at Airport To Kiss Presley Goodbye

By PAUL WILDER
Tribune Staff Writer

Only two of Elvis Presley's giggling girl friends were at Tampa International Airport to kiss him goodbye yesterday.

And they got there by mistake.

It was all supposed to have been a sort of super-hush-hush deal so the airport wouldn't be jammed and cause more trouble for already hijack-conscious airline personnel.

Up at 3 a.m.

But Jannette Tamborello, 15, of 602 N. MacDill and Linda Carlisi, 14, of 510 N. MacDill, got up at 3 a.m. to drive to Crystal River and see if they could have breakfast with their idol.

They are organizers of an Elvis Presley Fan Club in Tampa and have 150 members who write lett rs to the

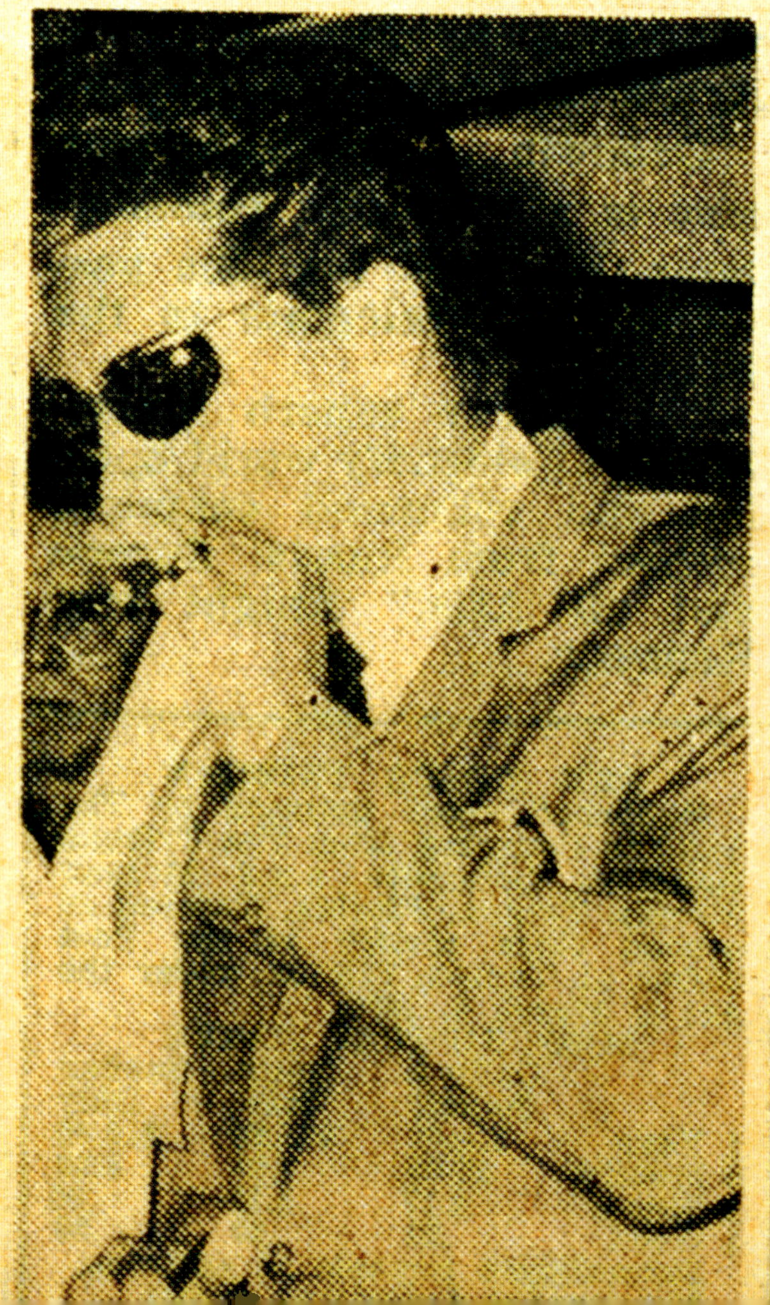

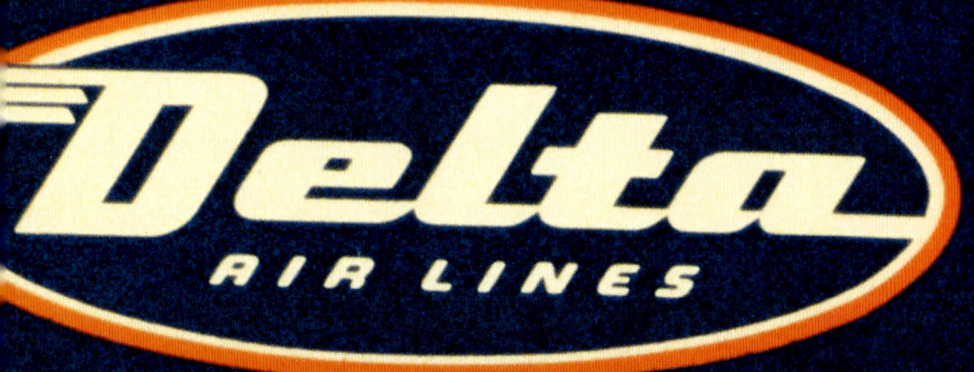

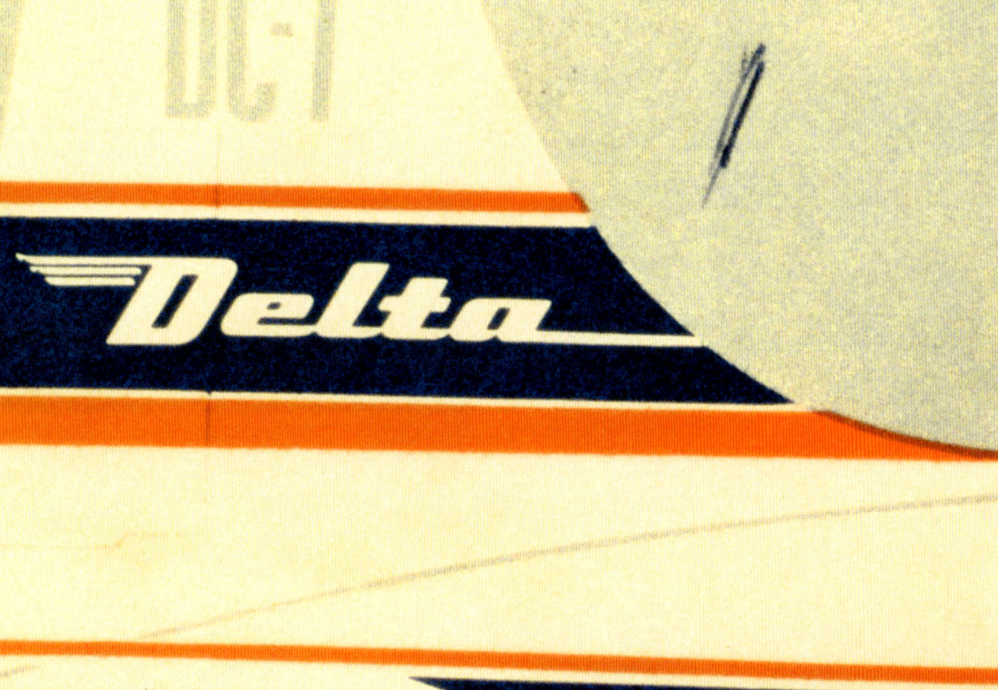

Detroit
Chicago
St Louis
Cincinnati
New York/Newark
Washington
Memphis
Atlanta
Charlotte
Jacksonville
New Orleans
Miami
Havana
San Juan

FARE 35.15
EQUIVALENT AMOUNT PAID
TAX 3.52
TOTAL 38.67
FORM OF PAYMENT

F

NAME OF PASSENGER Elvis Pressley

TO Memphis Houston

DAL 455 6/12

NOT TRANSFERABLE

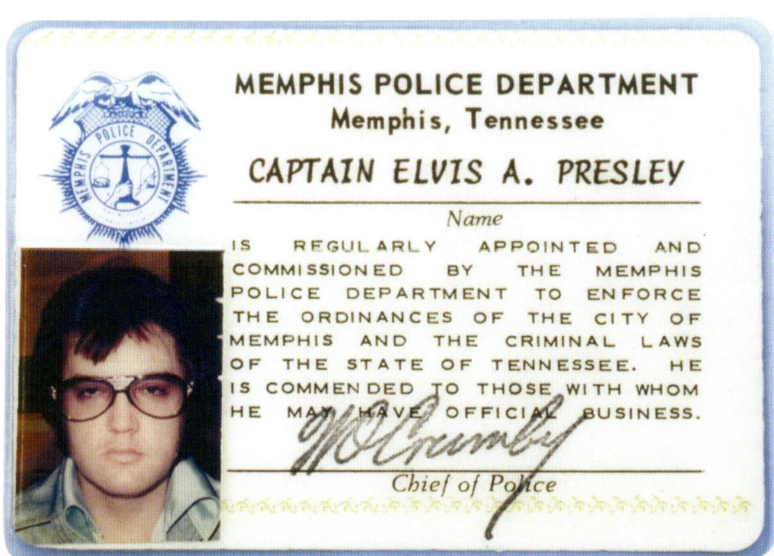
MEMPHIS POLICE DEPARTMENT
Memphis, Tennessee

CAPTAIN ELVIS A. PRESLEY

Name

IS REGULARLY APPOINTED AND COMMISSIONED BY THE MEMPHIS POLICE DEPARTMENT TO ENFORCE THE ORDINANCES OF THE CITY OF MEMPHIS AND THE CRIMINAL LAWS OF THE STATE OF TENNESSEE. HE IS COMMENDED TO THOSE WITH WHOM HE MAY HAVE OFFICIAL BUSINESS.

Chief of Police

Captain Elvis Memphis Police Badge
Elvis was a reserve Captian on the Memphis Police force. He had great respect for Law Enforcement and even once said that if he had not become an entertainer, he wanted to be a police officer.

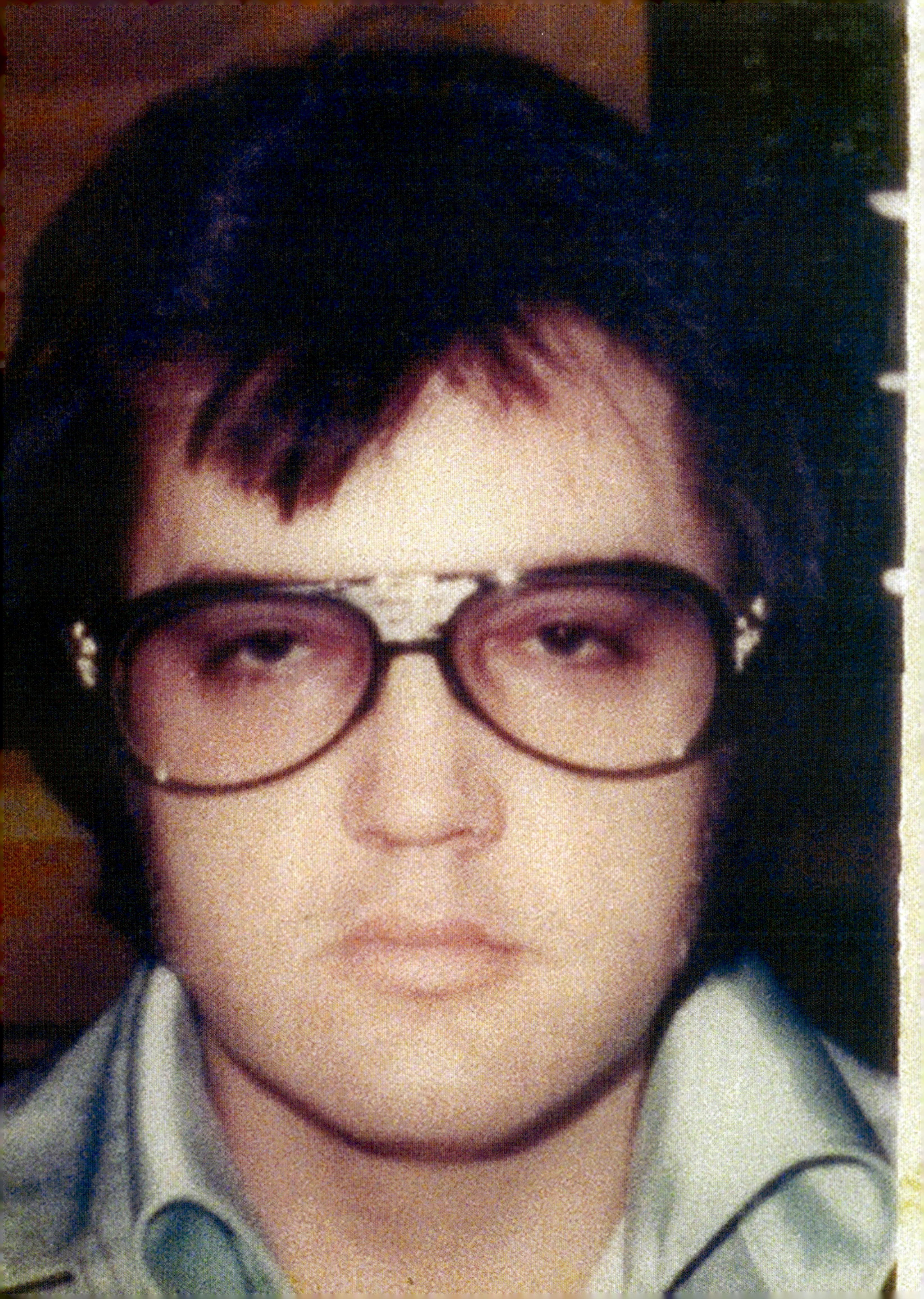

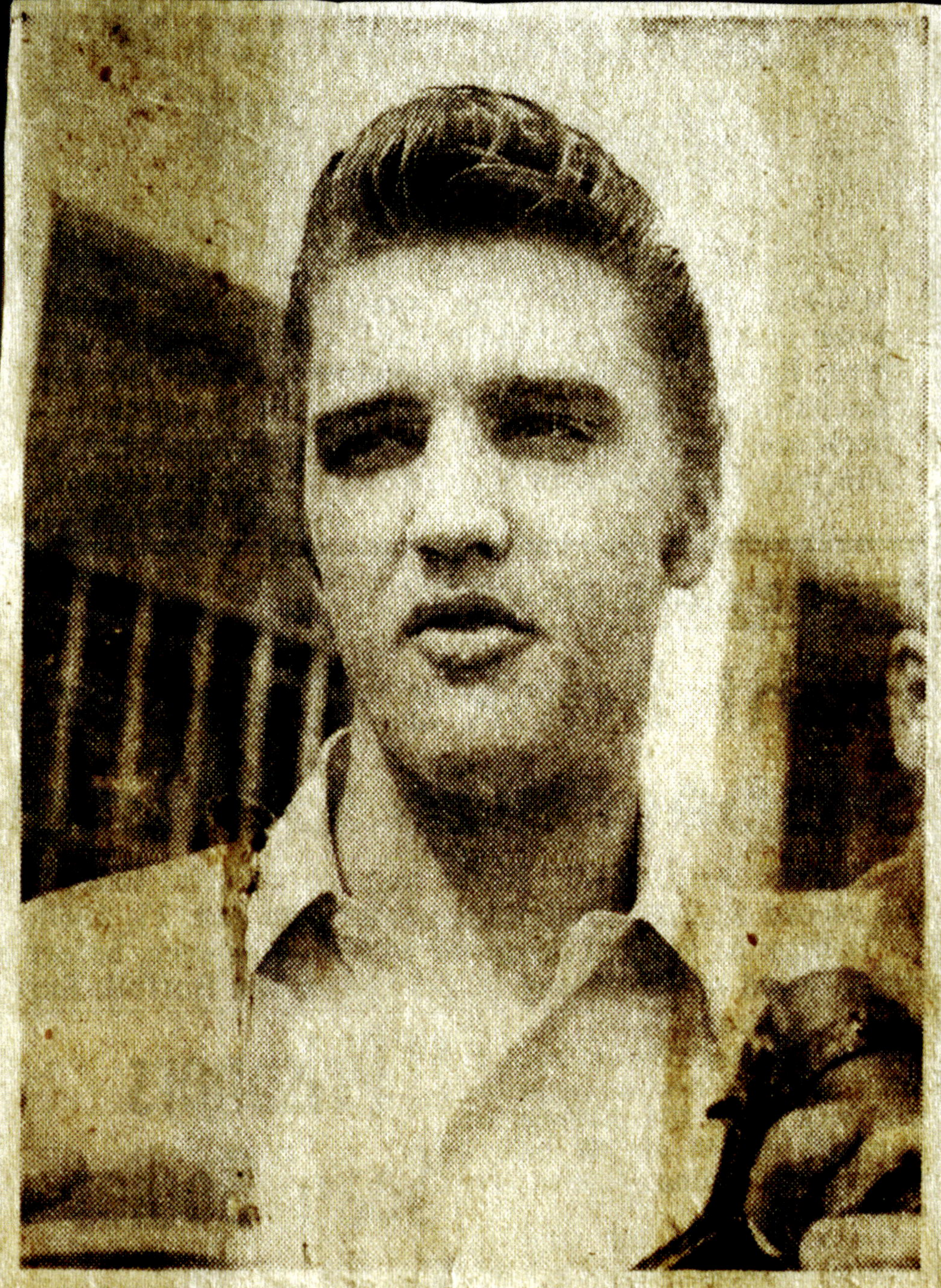

ELVIS THE MAN—Collar open, tie hanging loose and badly in need of a haircut, this is Elvis Presley, the singer who has captured America's youth in much the same fashion as did Rudy Vallee and Frank Sinatra in past years. The 21-year-old former Tupelo, Miss., truck driver answers critics who say he "can't carry a tune in a bucket" with his $1,000,000 bank-roll, his fleet of flashy automobiles and his great following, The Teenager. Dubbed "Elvis the Pelvis" because of his unorthodox if not sensual body movements while howling rock n' roll lyrics, Presley has skyrocketed to the top of the entertainment world. Critics feel he will skid just as fast.

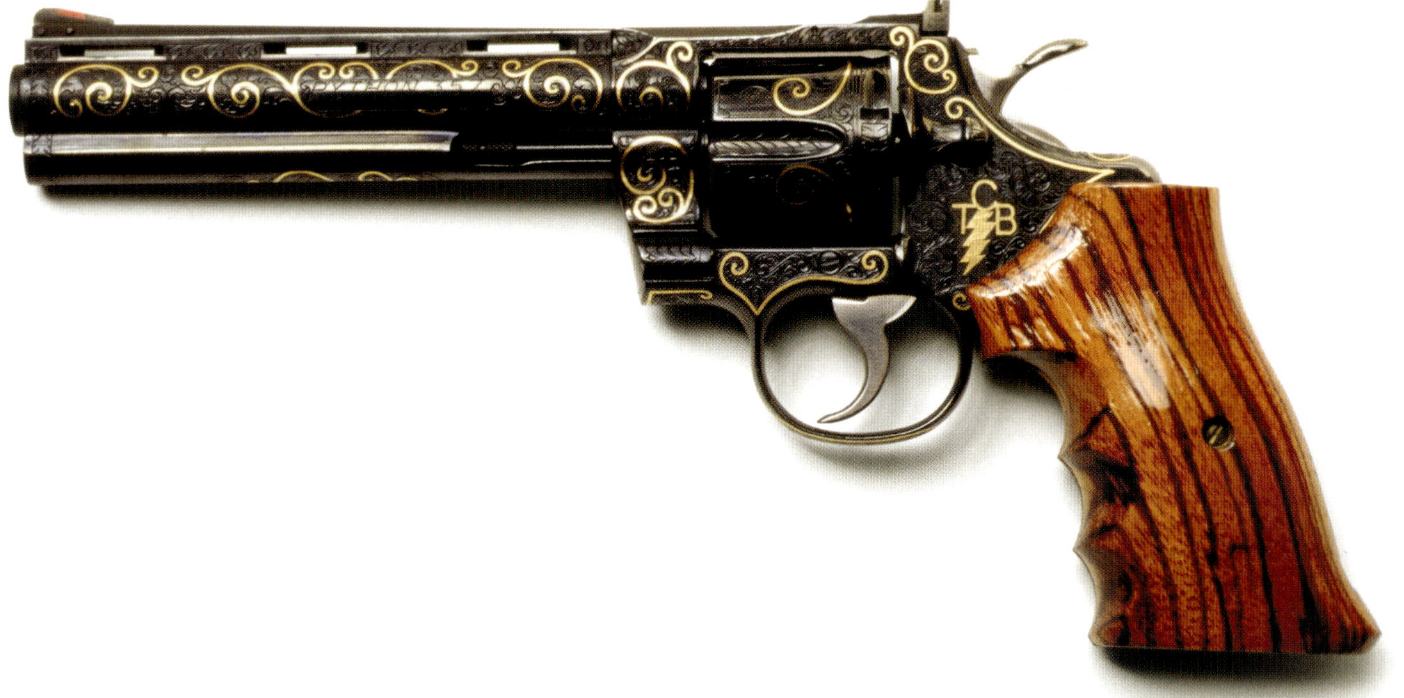

TCB Revolver
A Colt .357 Python revolver with the Taking Care of Business logo.

PRECISION
MEMPHIS
409-52-2002
ELVIS PRESLEY

PRECISION

MEMPHIS

409-52-2002

78 ELVIS PRESLEY

STATEMENT OF EMPLOYEE'S EAR

HOURS	DATE PERIOD ENDING	EARNINGS		
		REGULAR	OVERTIME	OTHER
40.00	MAR 15'54	62.00		

DETACH BEFORE CASHING

RETAIN THIS STATEMENT. IT IS YOUR RECEIPT FOR FEDERAL TAXES AND OTHER DEDUCTIONS

DATE PERIOD ENDING
R 15'54
DETACH BEFORE CASHING
AIN THIS STATEMENT. IT IS YOUR RECEIPT
FEDERAL TAXES AND OTHER DEDUCTIONS

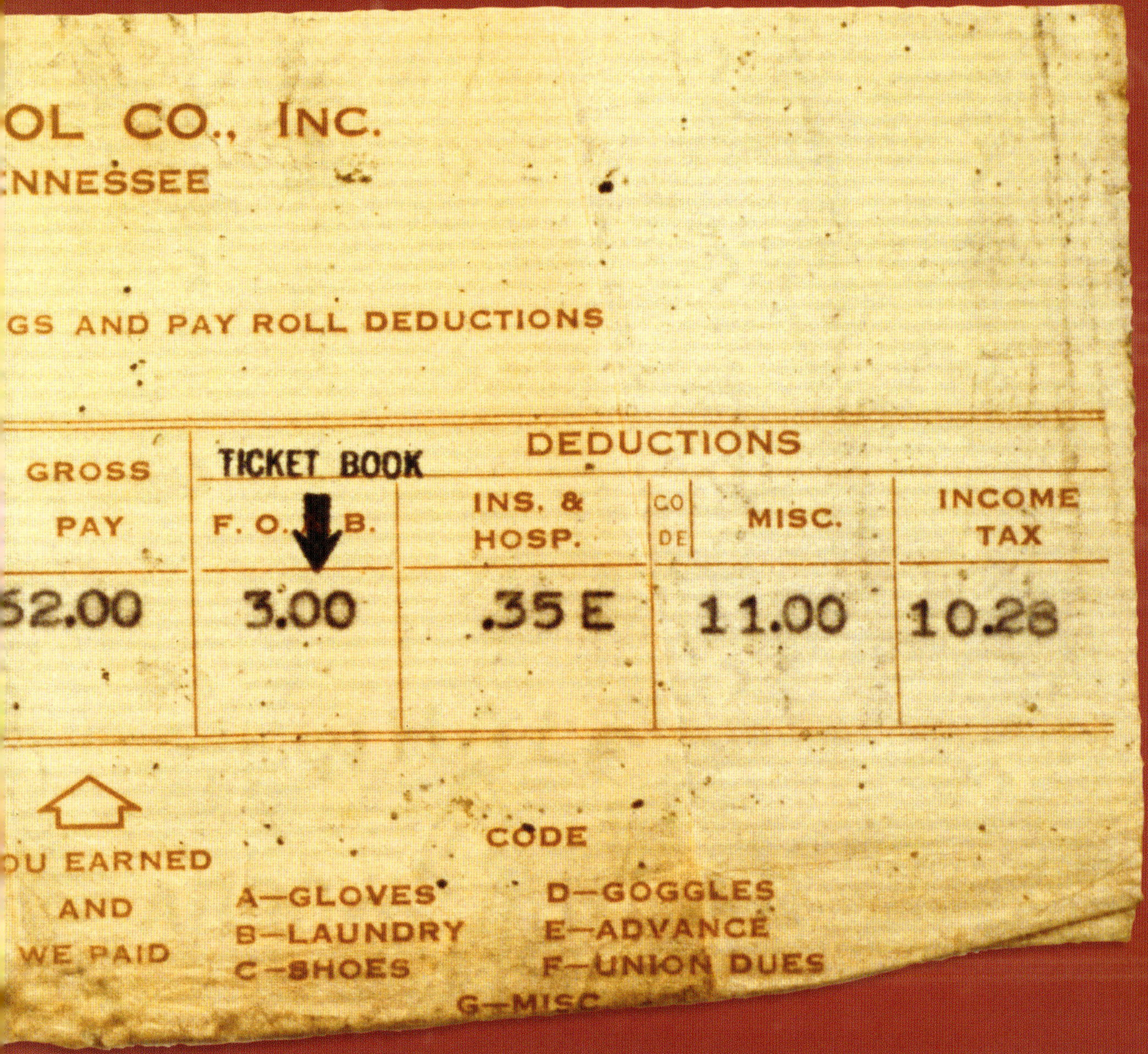

OL CO., INC.
NNESSEE

GS AND PAY ROLL DEDUCTIONS

GROSS PAY	TICKET BOOK F. O. B.	DEDUCTIONS INS. & HOSP.	CODE	MISC.	INCOME TAX
52.00	3.00	.35	E	11.00	10.28

OU EARNED AND WE PAID

CODE

A—GLOVES
B—LAUNDRY
C—SHOES
D—GOGGLES
E—ADVANCE
F—UNION DUES
G—MISC

Precision Tool Company Paycheck
A pay stub from one of Elvis's truck driving jobs, before he began recording.

ALL STAR SHOWS
P.O. Box 417
Tour No. ____________

87-530
641

MADISON, TENN., Feb. 27 1956 No. 798

PAY TO THE ORDER OF ELVIS PRESLEY $5000.00

------FIVE THOUSAND & 00/100---------------------------- DOLLARS

ADVANCE PAYMENT ON EARNINGS.. ELVIS PRESLEY SHOW
TOUR FEB. 5-26, 1956.

FOR ____________

MADISON BRANCH
FIRST AMERICAN NATIONAL BANK
OF NASHVILLE
MADISON, TENNESSEE

Colonel Tom Parker

HARLAND P-1

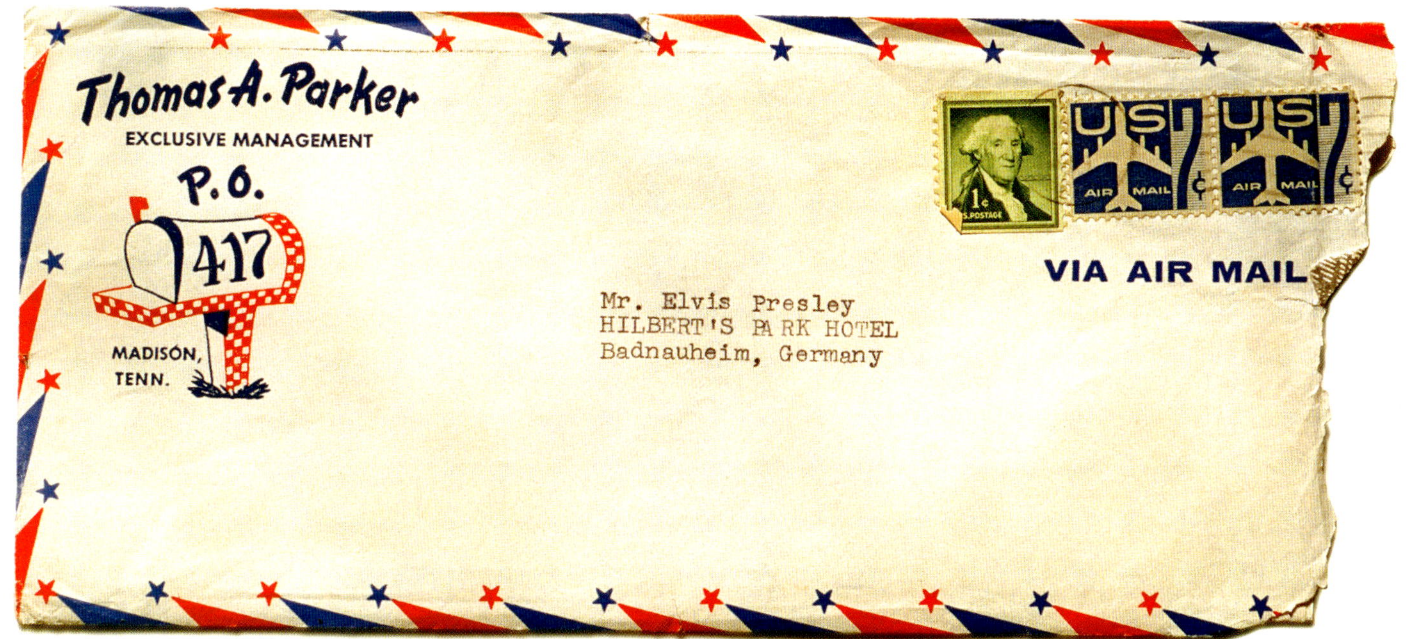

Envelope
Addressed to Elvis from the Colonel while he was in Germany.

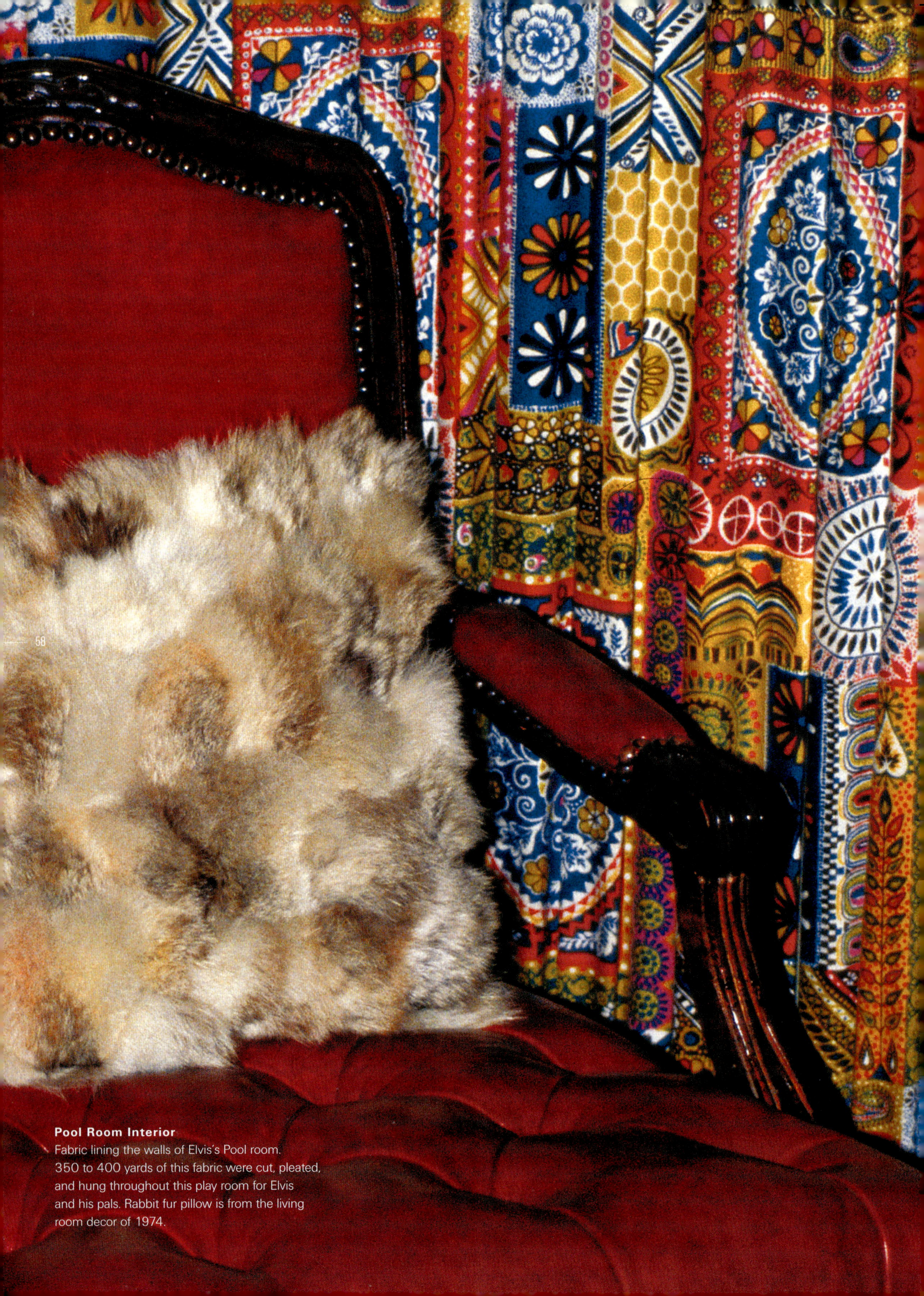

Pool Room Interior
Fabric lining the walls of Elvis's Pool room. 350 to 400 yards of this fabric were cut, pleated, and hung throughout this play room for Elvis and his pals. Rabbit fur pillow is from the living room decor of 1974.

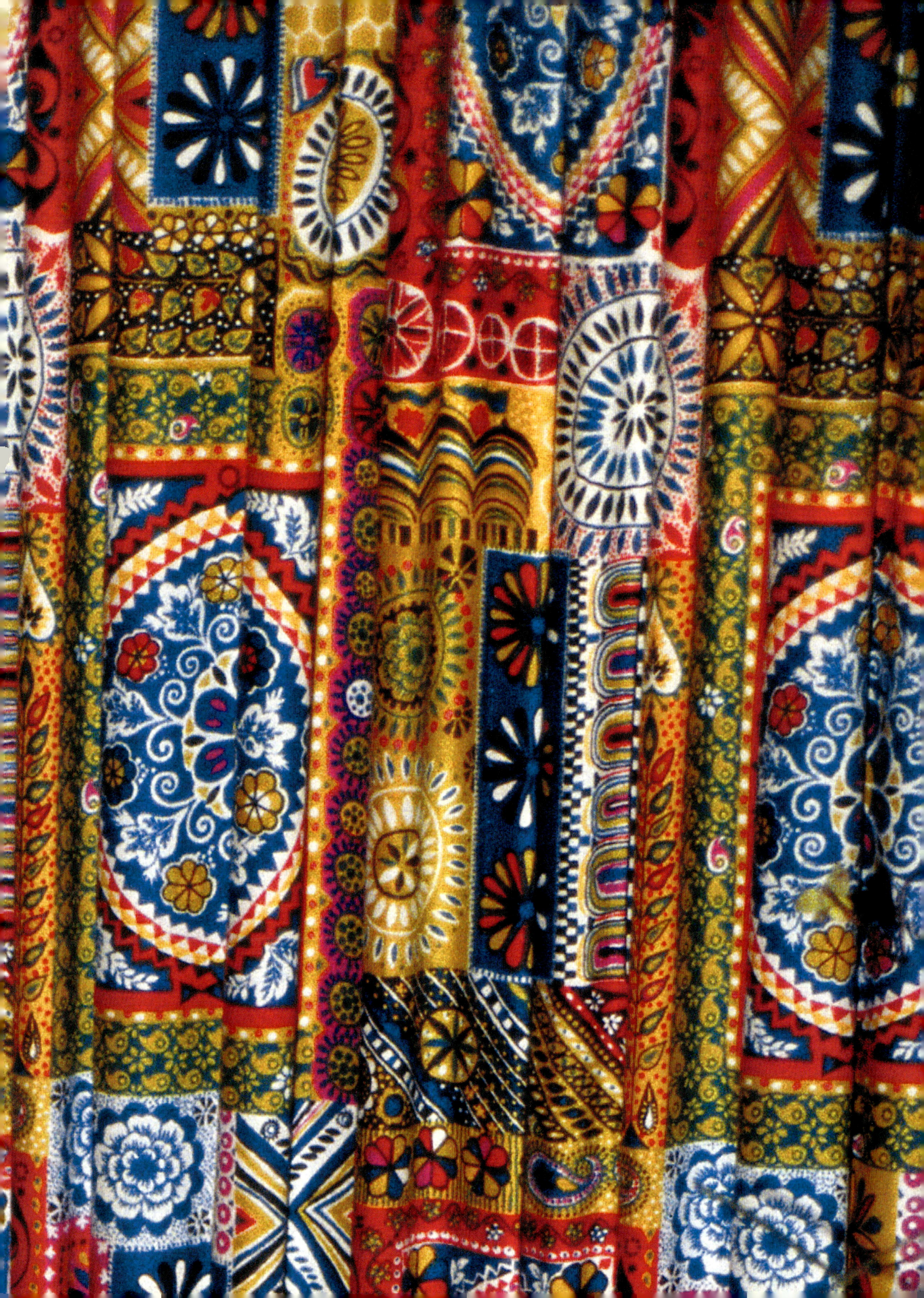

Jungle Room Interiors
Elvis came upon this Polynesian decor at Donald's furniture store in Memphis in 1974. The Jungle Room, as it was later named, was a favorite hangout for Elvis and his friends.

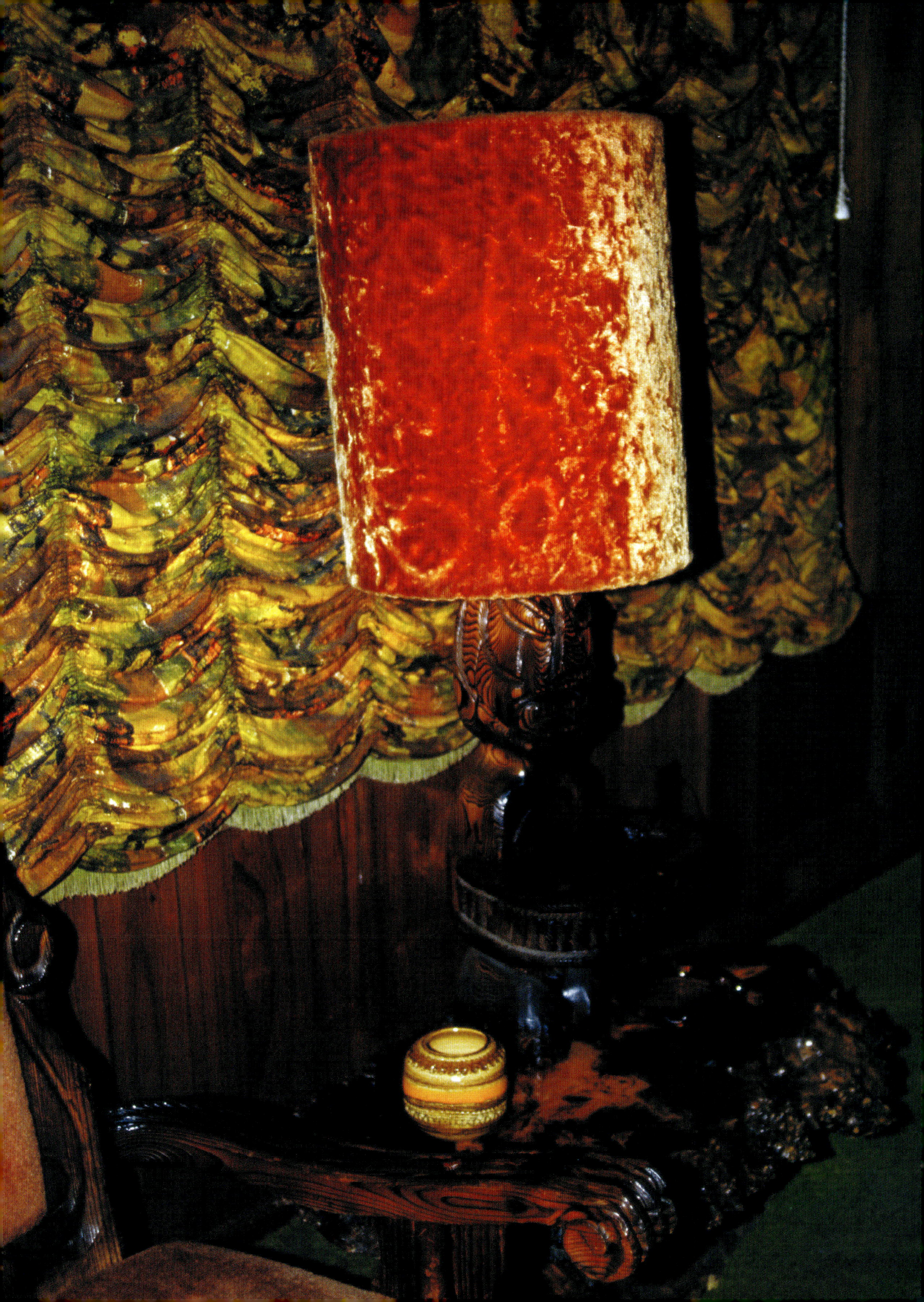

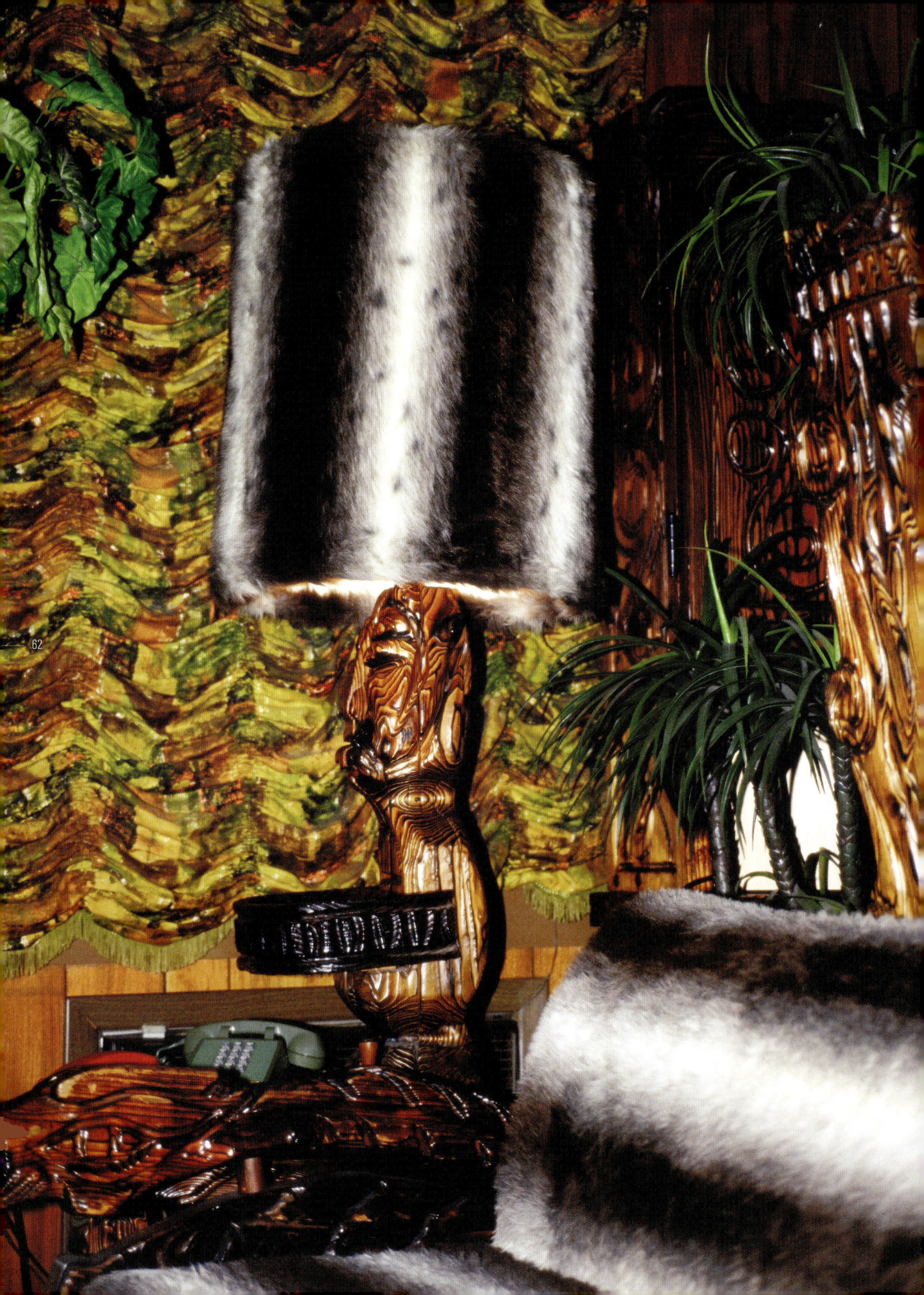

Jungle Room Lamp
A fur-covered lamp purchased
by Elvis at Donald's furniture store,
Memphis, Tennessee.

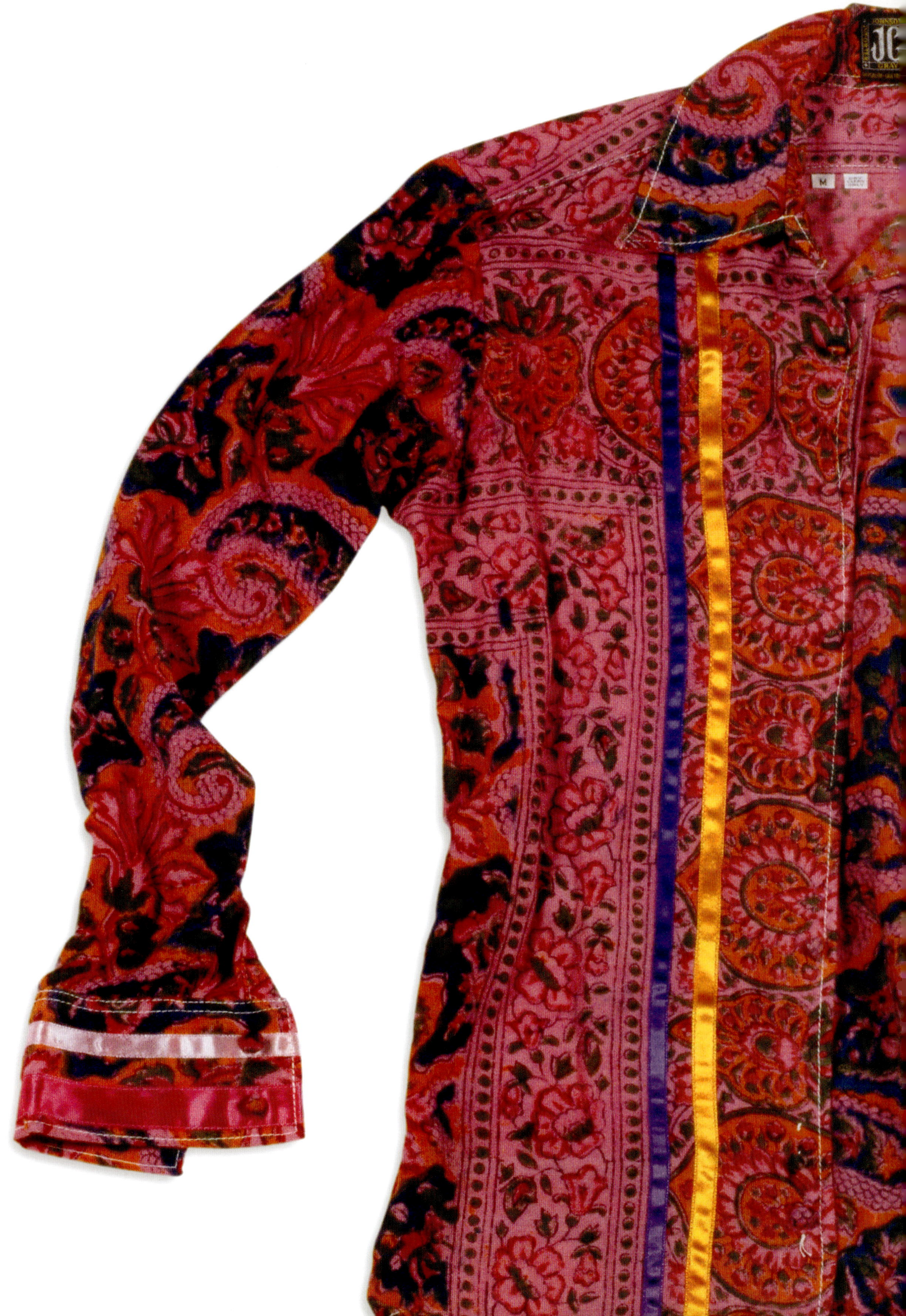

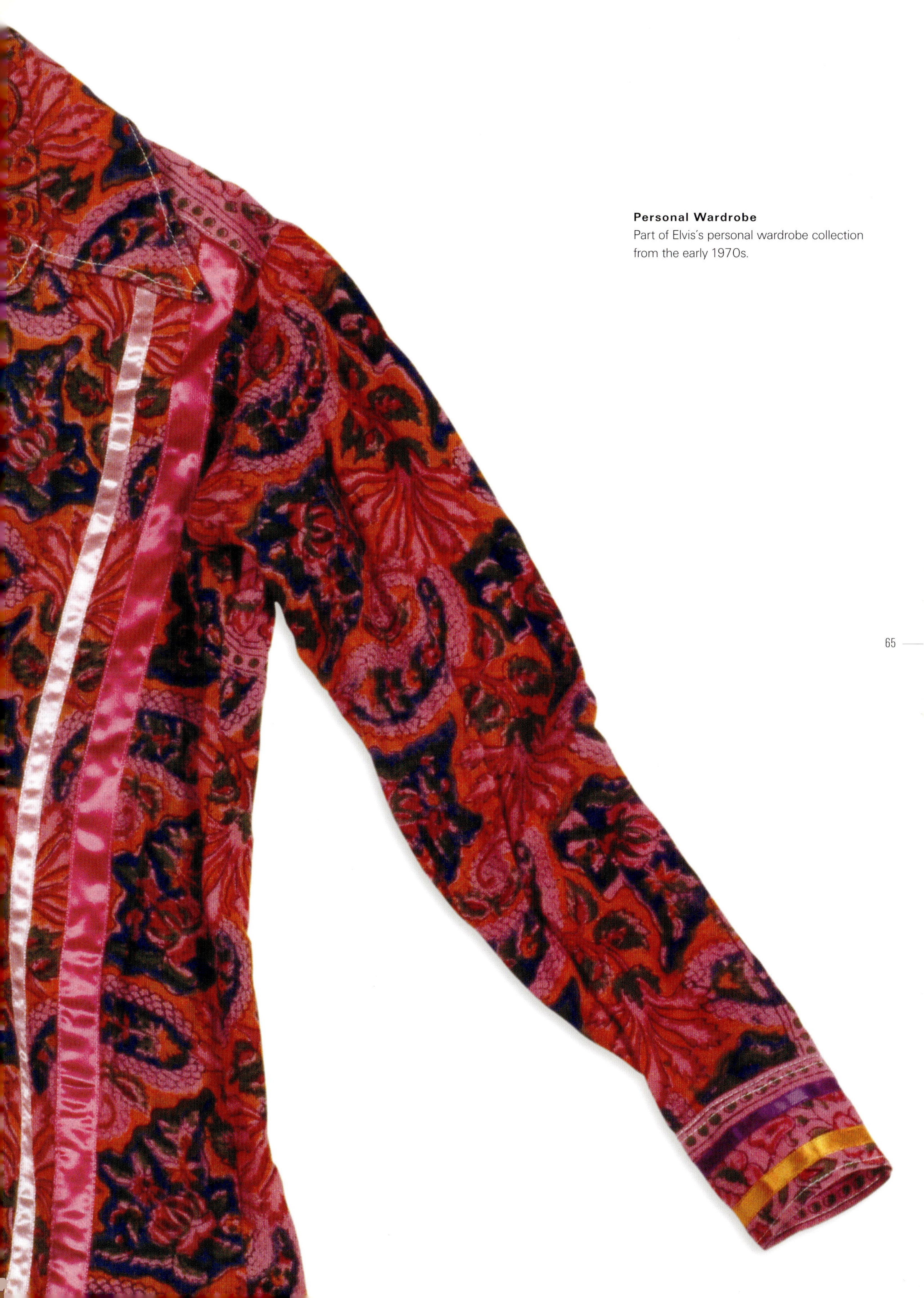

Personal Wardrobe
Part of Elvis's personal wardrobe collection from the early 1970s.

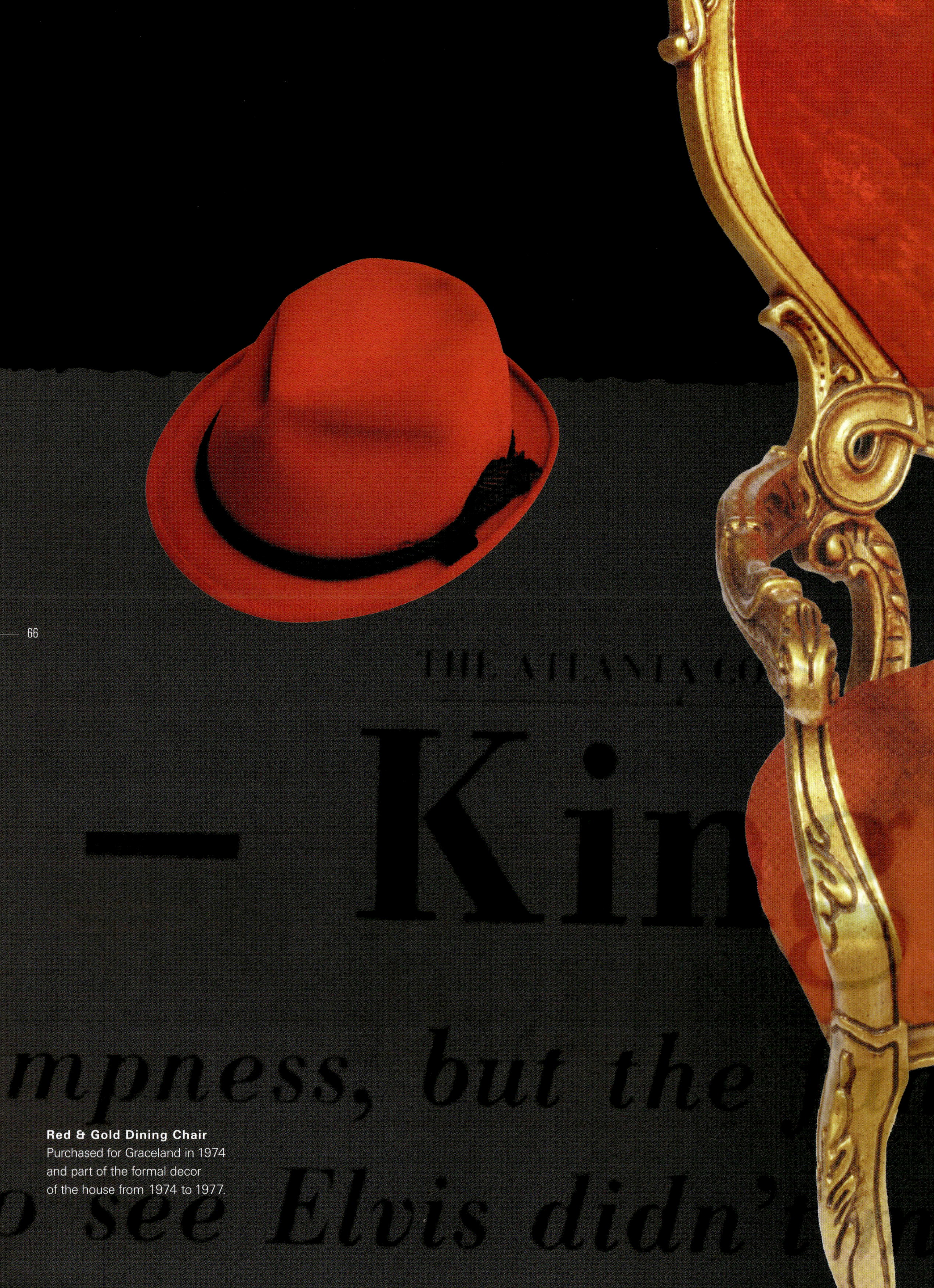

Red & Gold Dining Chair
Purchased for Graceland in 1974 and part of the formal decor of the house from 1974 to 1977.

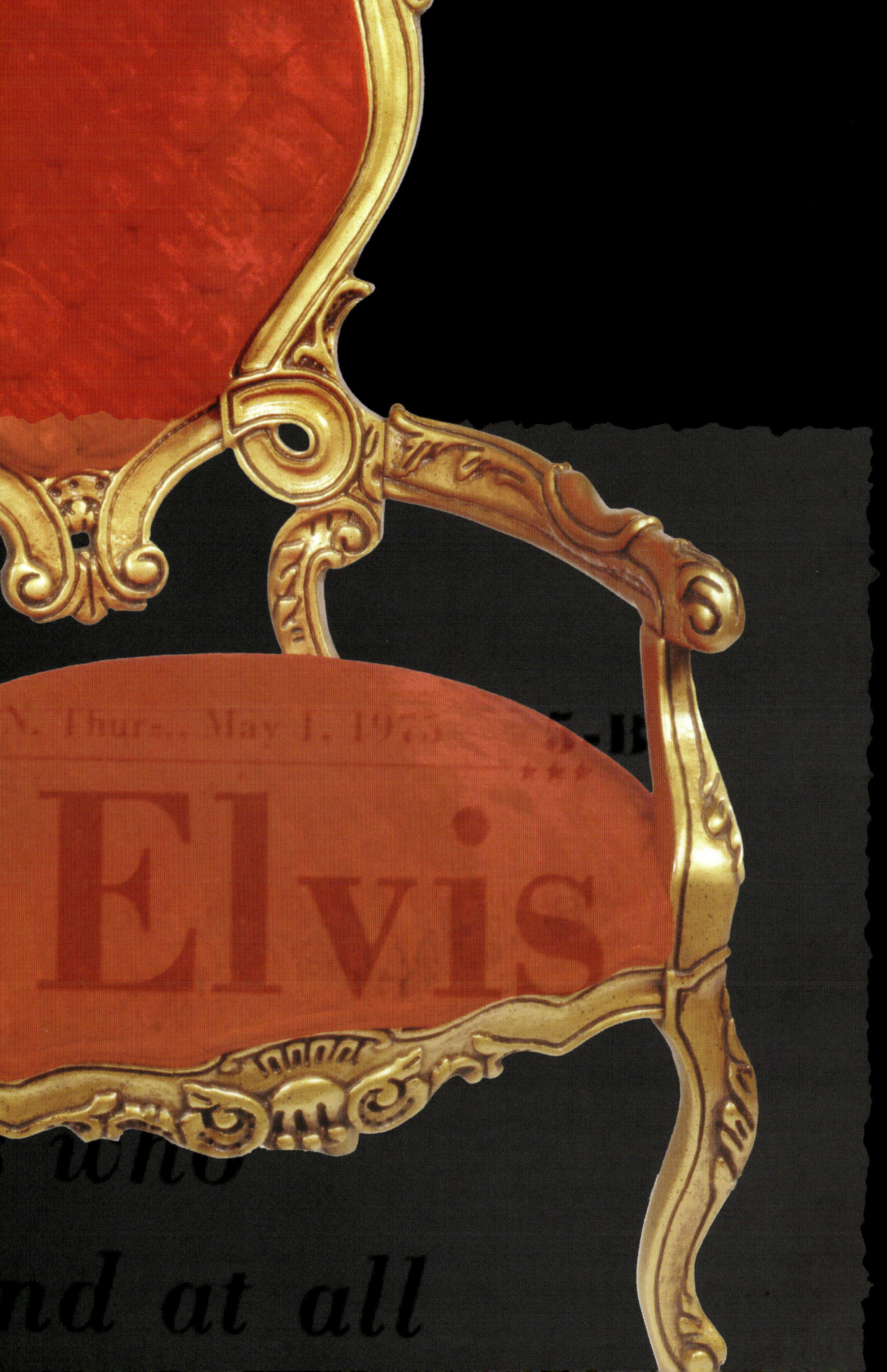
Thurs., May 1, 1975
Elvis
who
at all

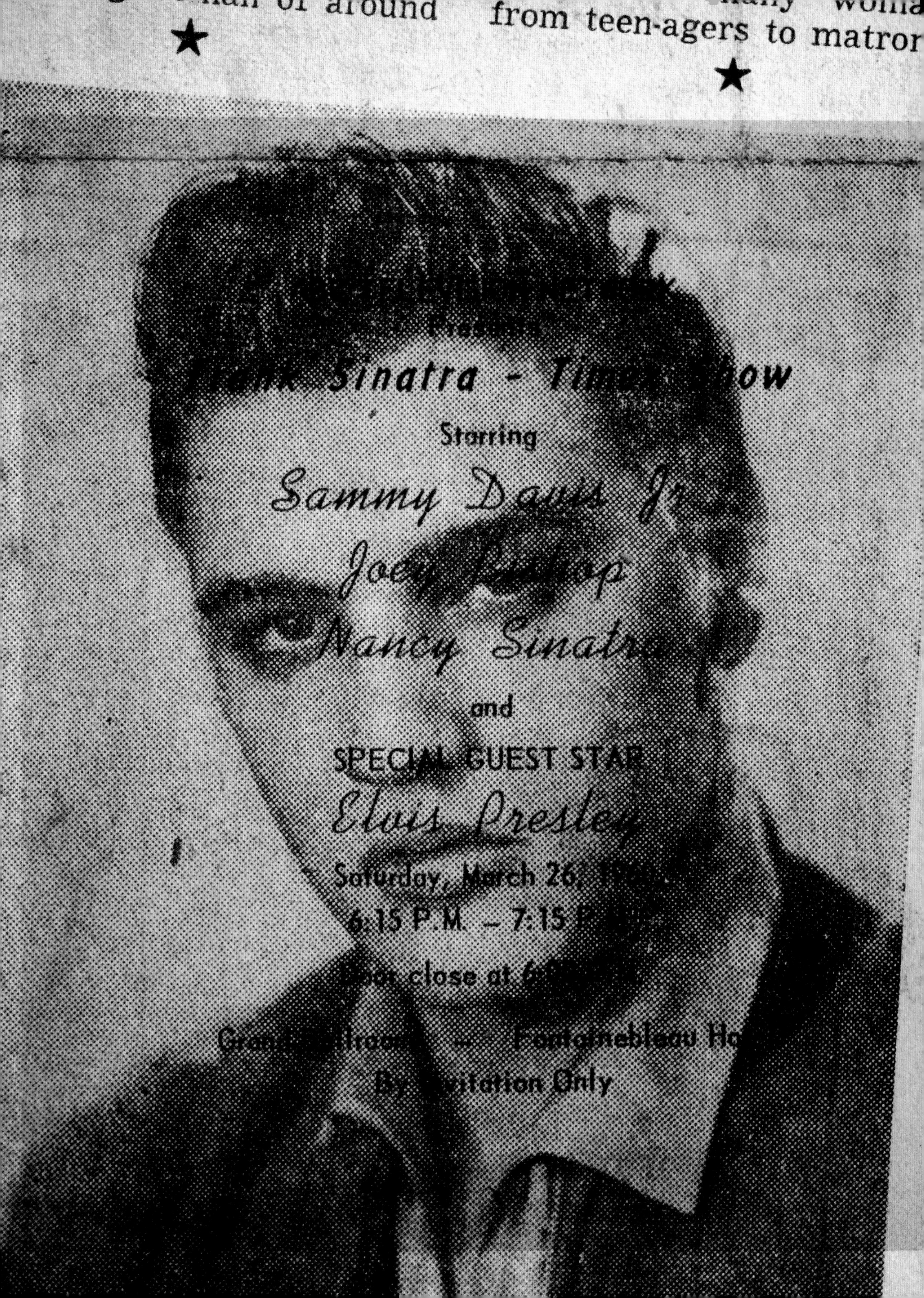

from teen-agers to matron
Sinatra -
Starring
Sammy Davis
Nancy Sinatra
and
SPECIAL GUEST STAR
Elvis Presley
Saturday, March 26,
6:15 P.M. – 7:15
close at
By Invitation Only

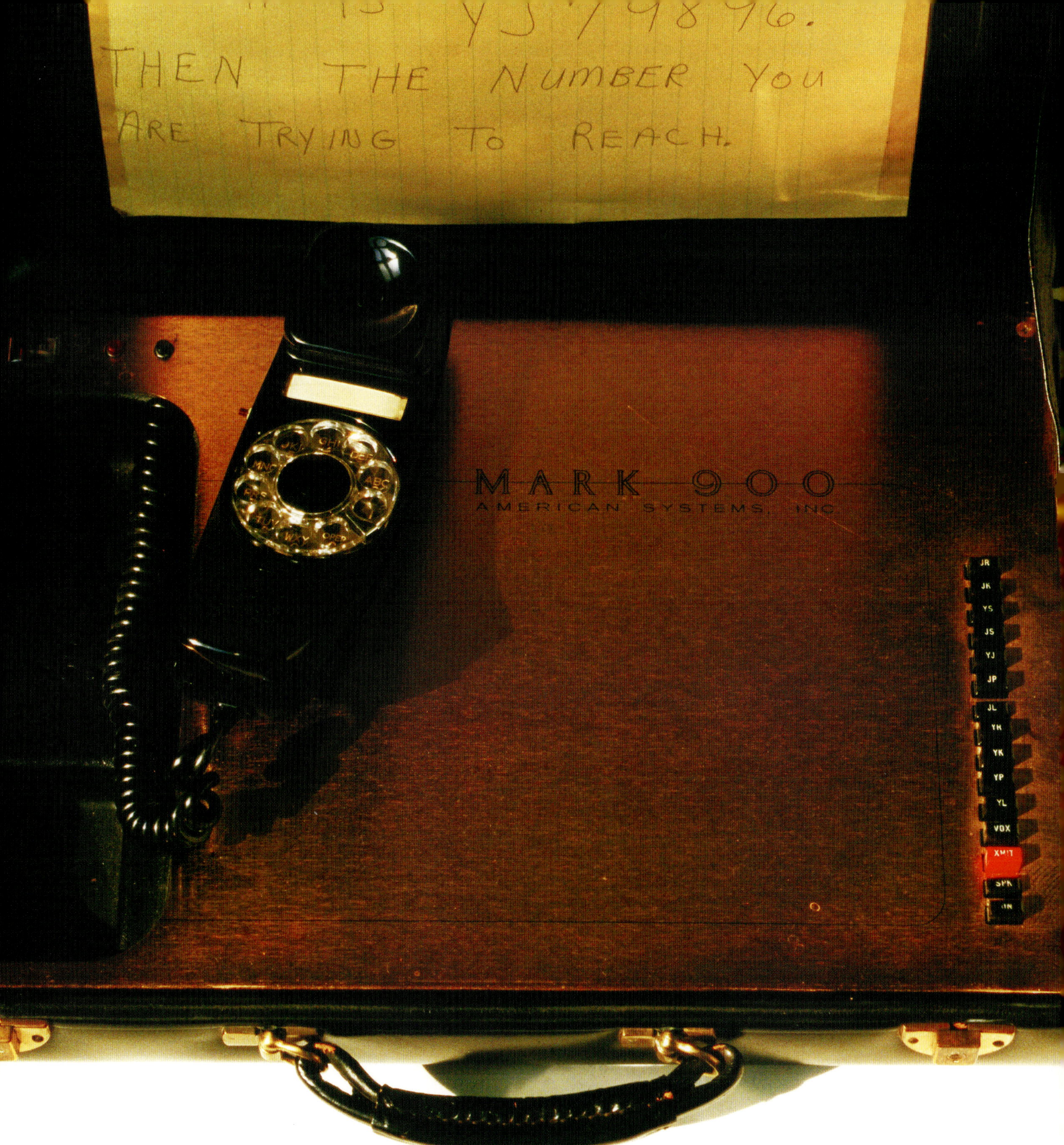

Mobile Phone

Before cell phones, Elvis was carrying this briefcase phone. A man on the cutting edge of technology, Elvis loved gadgets.

Elvis Just Average Abnormal American

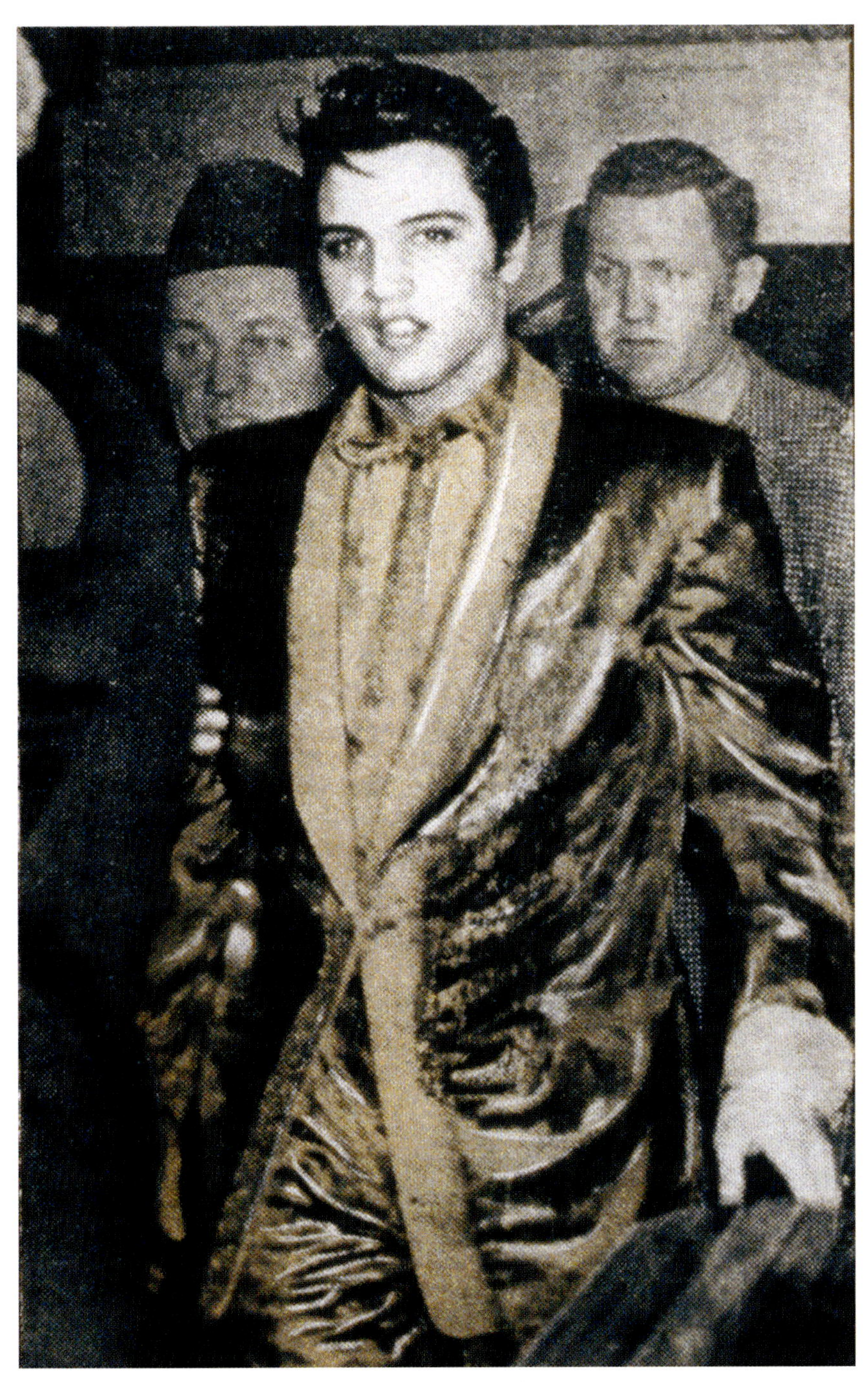

Security
A photopolymer gravure etching of Elvis in his gold lamé suit, circa 1957.

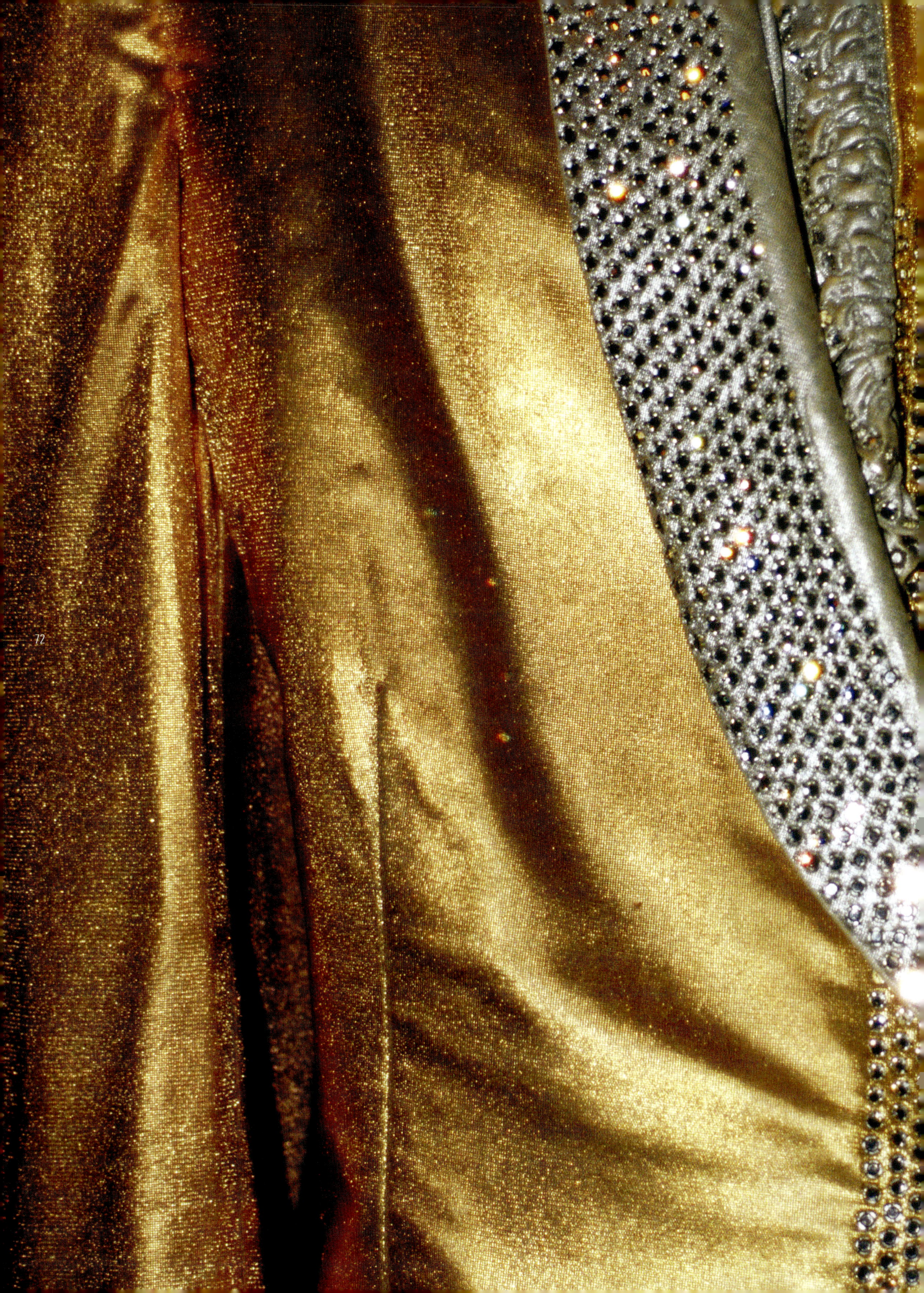

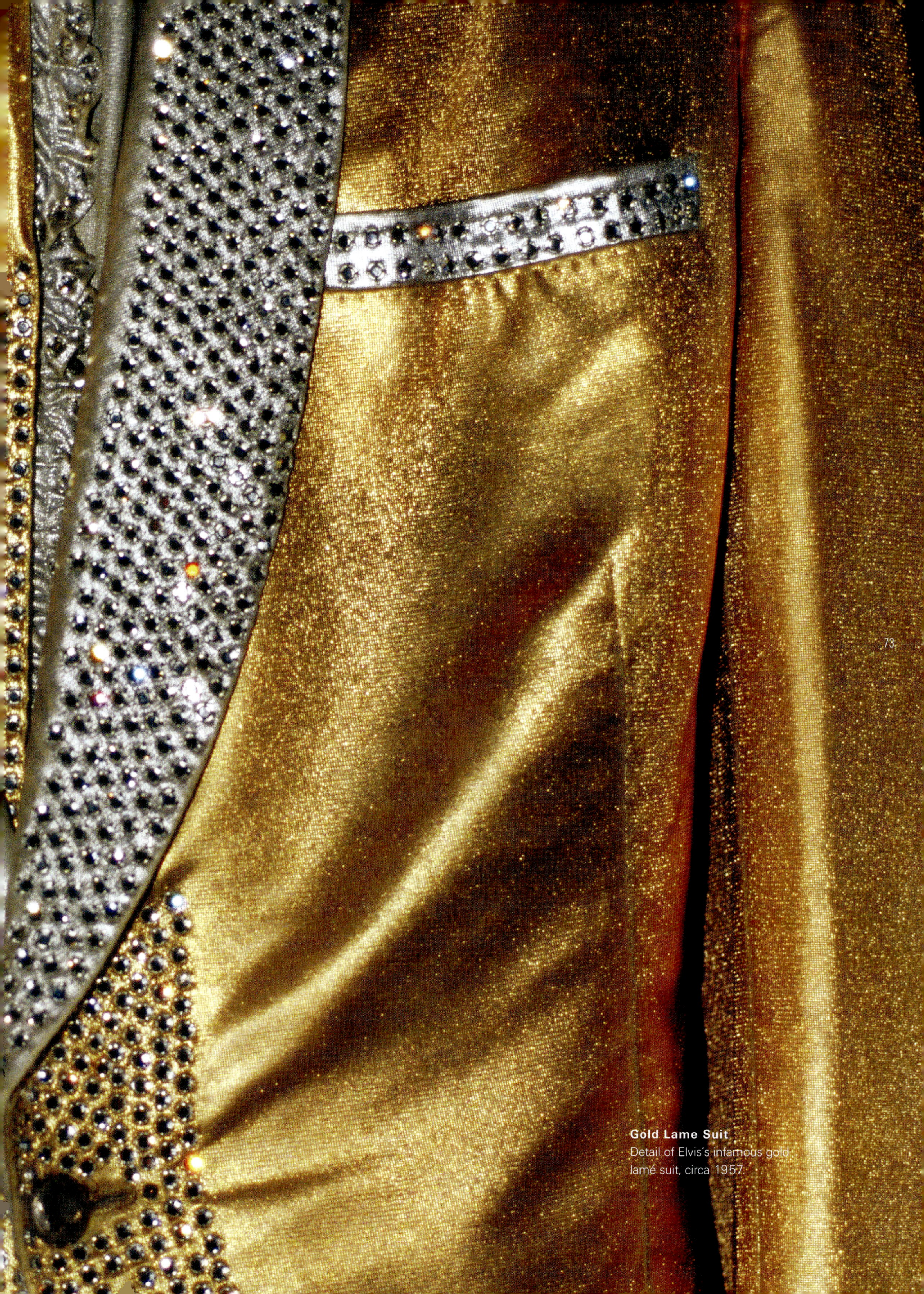

Gold Lame Suit
Detail of Elvis's infamous gold lamé suit, circa 1957.

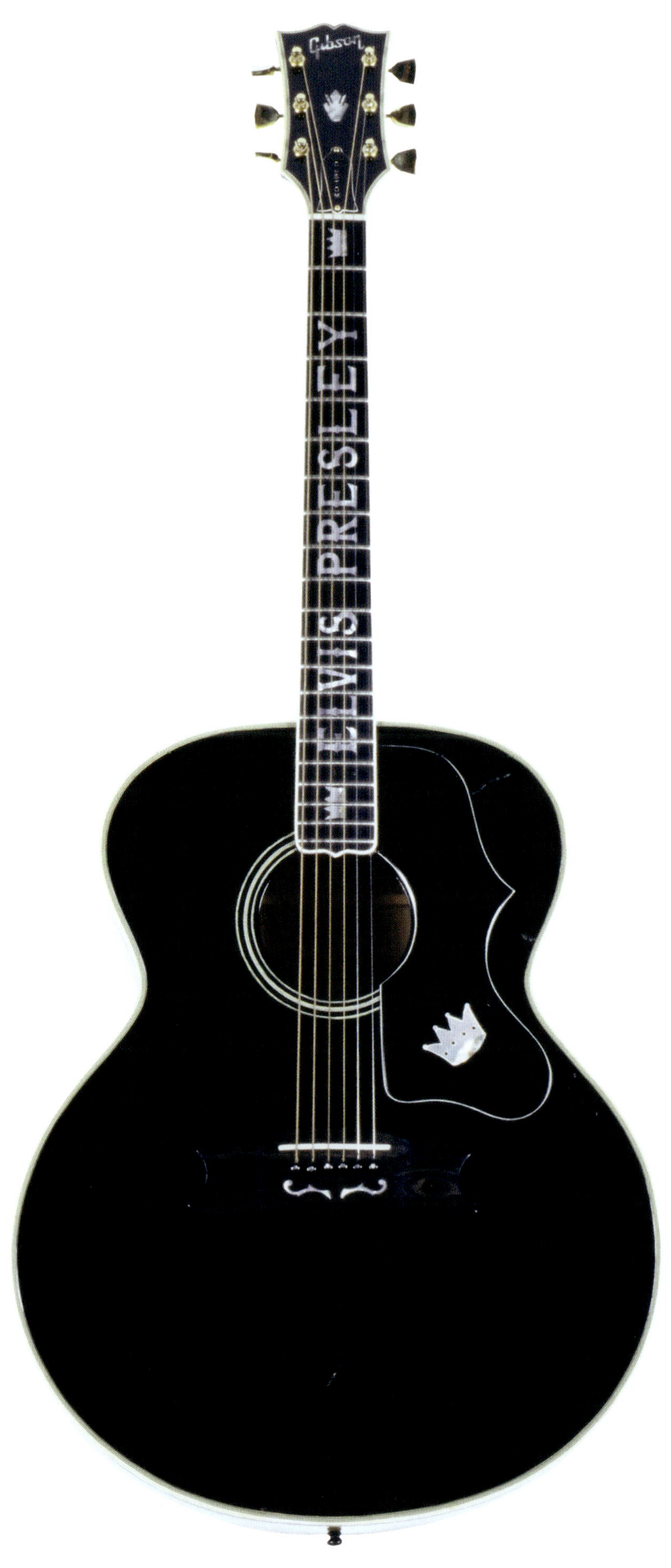

Black Guitar (With "Elvis Presley" Inlaid In Neck)
A Gibson J-200 used by Elvis onstage in the mid-1970s.

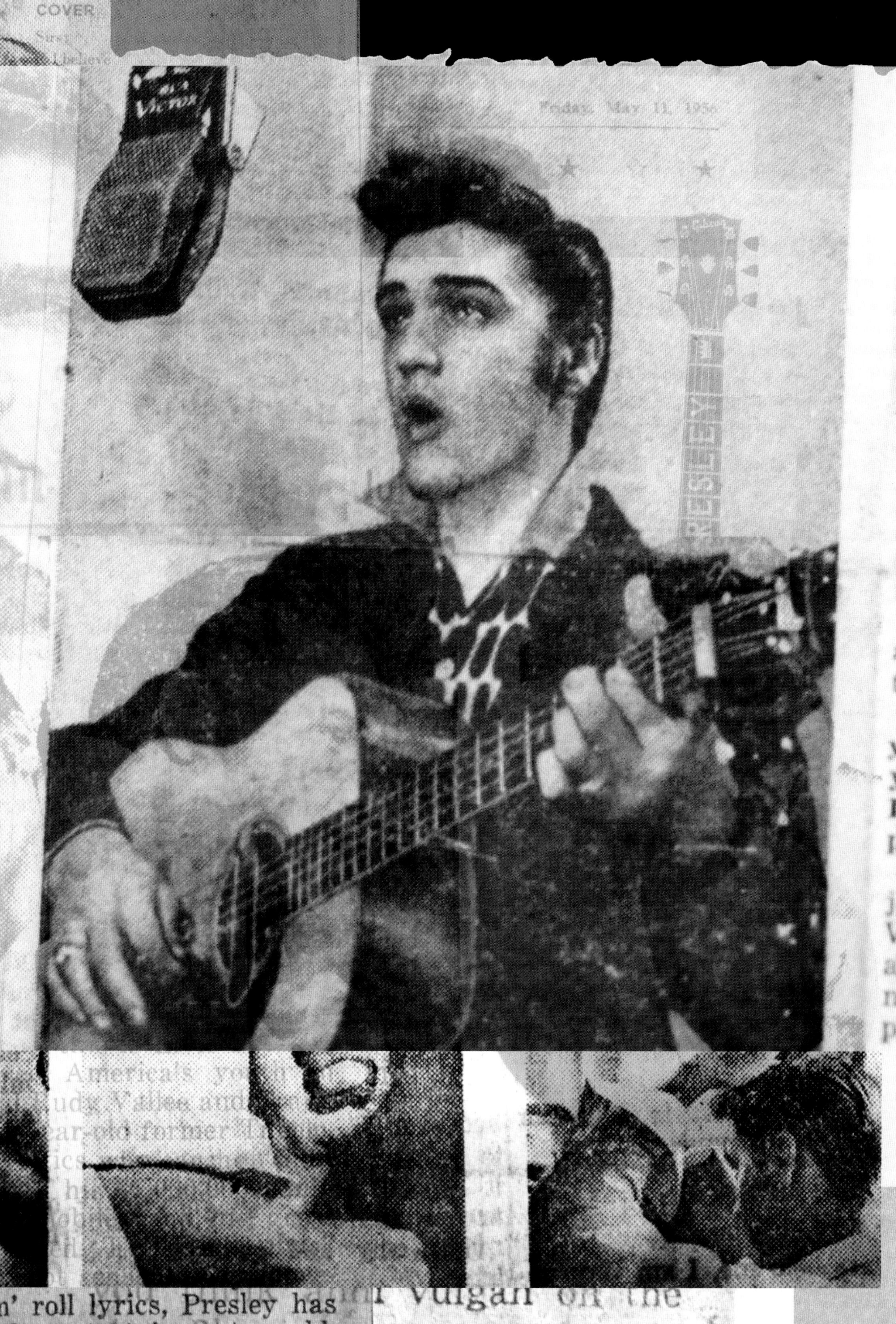

COVER

Friday, May 11, 1956

seen a
Vict
about
the old
Presley
plunke

SINCE
an
Victor
ting the
is consi
field, w
His
while t
lists, bu
sold in
market.
"Hea
and ano
the half

Presl
you get
you con
I have
played i
He sa
jockeys
Victor i
also add
newer re
publicati

n' roll lyrics, Presley has
the entertainment world.
t as fast.

vulgar on the

"Son," she said, 'You're not

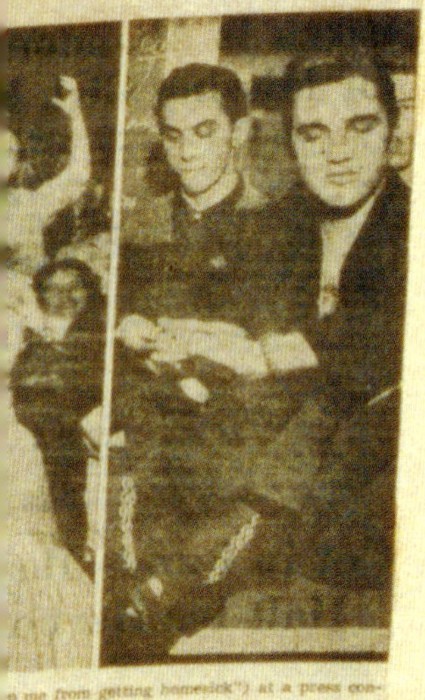

...p me from getting homesick") at a press con-... the show.

THE OREGONIAN, TUESDAY, SEPTEMBER 3, 1957

...ic of Elvis Convinced ... Must Have Something'

Teener Tells Elvis Story

BY HOLLY JOHNSON

76

ELVIS SIN...

STADIUM EDITION

Oregon Journal

Section 1 PORTLAND, OR., MON., SEPT. 2, 1957 PRICE 5c

Presley First Began Singing As Youngster

Heartbreak Hotel First Top Record

Elvis Aron Presley, a phenomenon of show business, began singing as a youngster when his father bought him a $2.98 ...

He was born in Tupelo, Miss., on January 8, 1935. The Presleys moved to Memphis, Tenn. in 1948, and Elvis graduated from L. C. Humes high school.

WHILE HE was still in school he cut an amateur record titled "That's All Right, Mama," as a gift for his mother. The record elicited some response later when it was aired by a Memphis radio station.

But things didn't really start happening for the 6-foot, 175-pound entertainer until he met "Colonel" Thomas A. Parker, a shrewd and able promoter who had handled Eddie Arnold, Hank Snow, Gene Austin, Roy Acuff and Tex Ritter.

Elvis had a following at the time, but it centered around Jacksonville, Fla., where a disc jockey doubled as Presley's manager. Parker bought Elvis' contract in mid-1955, and by the start of the next year people began hearing about the lad with the itchy delivery, the twitchy pelvis and the guitar he slapped like a bongo drum.

THE YEAR 1956 became the year of the Houn' Dog. Elvis earned nearly $1,000,000 and by the end of the year around 4000 fan letters were being addressed to him each day.

His sideburns precipitated family conferences about haircuts. His hip swiveling earned him a mild dig from Ed Sullivan, but later he was signed up for a triple shot on Sullivan's show for an unprecedented $50,000.

"Heartbreak Hotel" was Presley's first golden platter —which means it sold over 1,000,000 copies. Four others followed — "Houn' Dog," "I Want You, I Need You, I Love You," "Don't Be Cruel" and "Love Me Tender."

From a $35-a-week truck driver in Memphis, Presley became a singing sensation and, inevitably, a movie star.

HIS LEGEND is already a-building, with reports that he owns four Cadillacs, including one $10,000 custom-built job with a telephone; a motorcycle that is the despair of his manager; a three-wheel German vehicle, and a home with a 25 by 50-foot swimming pool, a garage as big as some houses, a dog kennel and a barbeque pit.

Reports say that his home is full of teddy bears of every description and that he owns dozens of shirts that he has never worn.

He is said to favor black and dark blue, but he sometimes is seen in an outfit that might include black and gold silk slacks, pink nylon shirt, light green socks, white cotton jacket with black markings and black loafer shoes.

And a guitar.

Teenagers Took Elvis Off Truck

Elvis Presley's manager, "Colonel" Thomas A. Parker, says he and Elvis have been good for each other "but don't let anyone tell you I made the boy what he is.

"The kids are the ones who made Elvis," Parker asserts. "Without them, he'd still be driving a truck."

Rock Music 'Snappy'

The music that Elvis Presley slaps out of his guitar takes its toll. The rock 'n' roller with the abandoned style averages three broken guitar strings a performance.

Presley Creates Real Jam Session

When Elvis Presley made a homecoming appearance at Tupelo, Miss., last year, he was greeted by a crowd of 12,500 persons.

Guarding the platform on which Elvis performed were 57 state highway patrolmen, 35 national guardsmen and 30 local police and deputies from nearby towns.

Despite this, the crowd stampeded toward the singer. Newsmen and photographers were forced to climb up on the 5-foot-high stage to get out of the way.

Elvis Good 'Business'

Elvis Presley has quite a few fans in the advertising business, men who realize the influence of the rock 'n' roll singer.

Presley's biggest following is from the vast teenage horde that buys, according to estimates, a little more than half of all the phonograph records sold.

Every day, an estimated 10,000 more youngsters enter the 13 to 19-year age bracket. Advertisers say a survey shows that the teenage group has an average of $12.71 spending money each week.

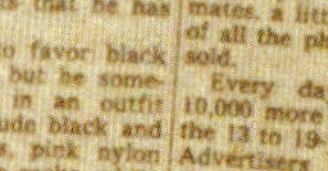

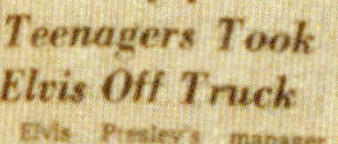

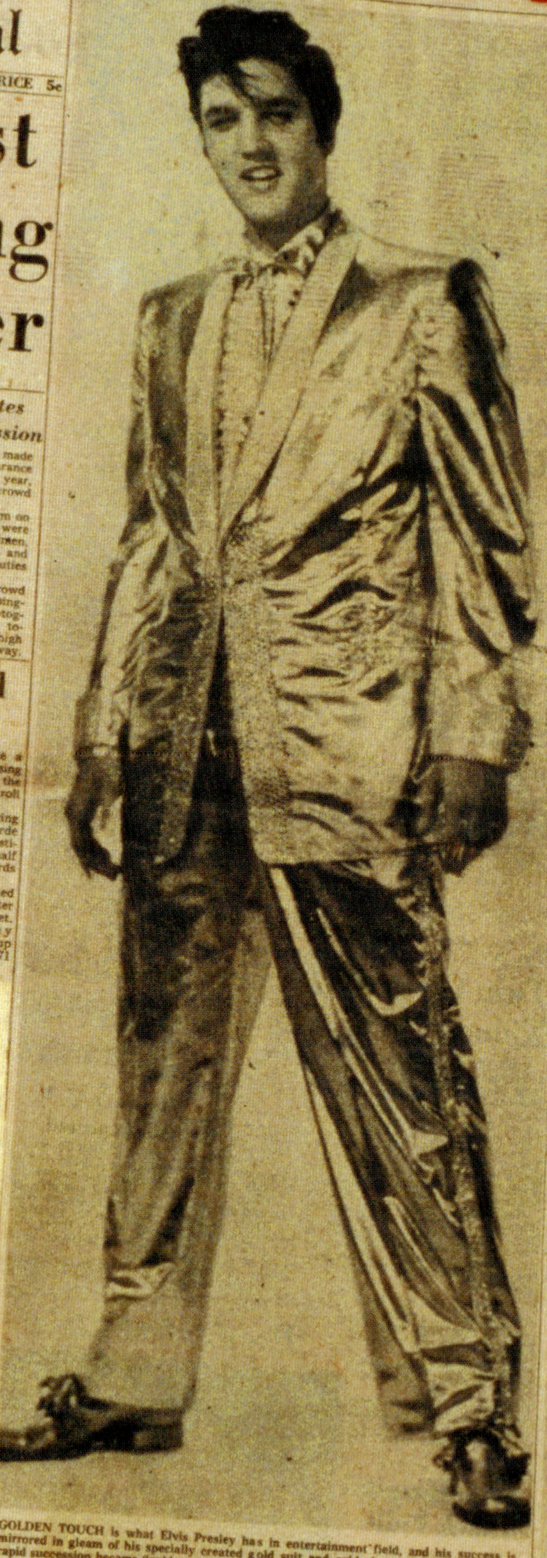

GOLDEN TOUCH is what Elvis Presley has in entertainment field, and his success is mirrored in gleam of his specially created gold suit and gold shoes. Five of his hits in rapid succession became "golden platters"—that is, sold over 1,000,000 copies.

School Bells Ring for Some Here

Thousands of Oregon children are enjoying the last day of the summer vacation Monday, facing a return to school rooms Tuesday.

But Portland pupils have a week's reprieve — classes in city schools do not open until Monday, September 9.

Schools in the Portland area which open Tuesday include Columbia, Gresham grade, Orient, Troutdale, Wilkes, Fairview, Bonny Slope, Skyline, Pleasant Valley, Sauvies Island, Springdale, Powell Valley, Rockwood, Lynch, Powellhurst, Holbrook and Bonneville.

WEDNESDAY OPENING is set for Corbett and Gilbert schools.

Along with Portland, schools to open next Monday include Parkrose, Gresham high, Whitaker, Russellville, Sylvan, Riverdale, David Douglas high and Beaverton.

Schools in Vancouver, Wash., get underway Wednesday.

Most Catholic schools open the 1957-58 term Tuesday, but some classes will be delayed because students are working in the bean and berry fields.

Indian Troops Ring Portuguese

NEW DELHI, Sept. 2—(AP)—Prime Minister Nehru said today India has moved troops around the small Portuguese colony of Daman on the west coast because the Portuguese have repeatedly fired across the border.

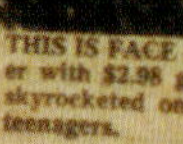

THIS IS FACE ... er with $2.98 ... skyrocketed on ... teenagers.

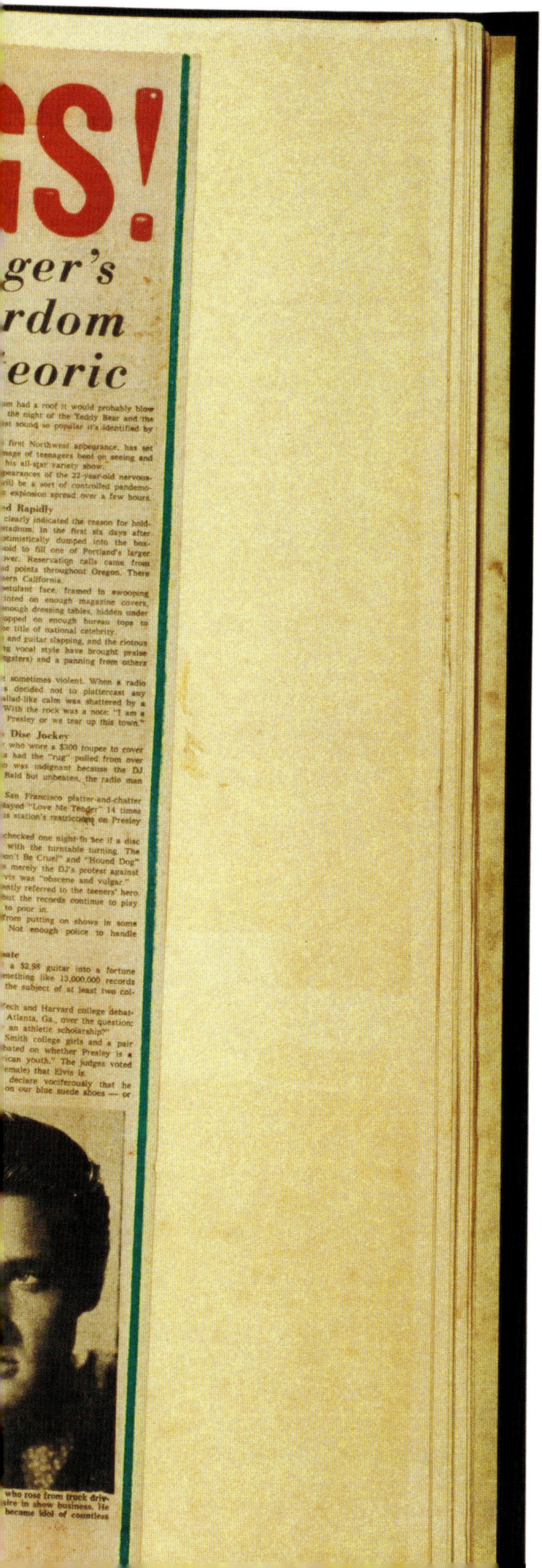

Elvis Scrapbook
Colonel Parker kept meticulous scrapbooks containing thousands of newspaper features and headlines, along with other personal notations.

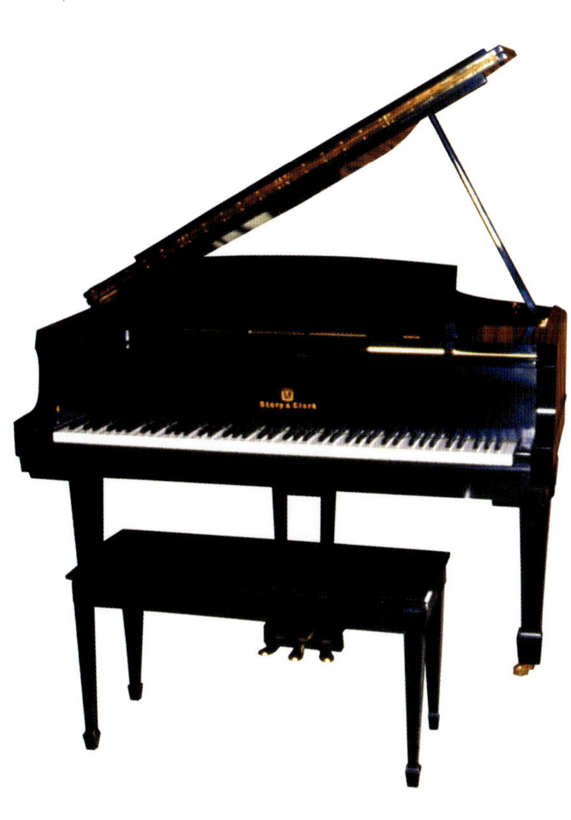

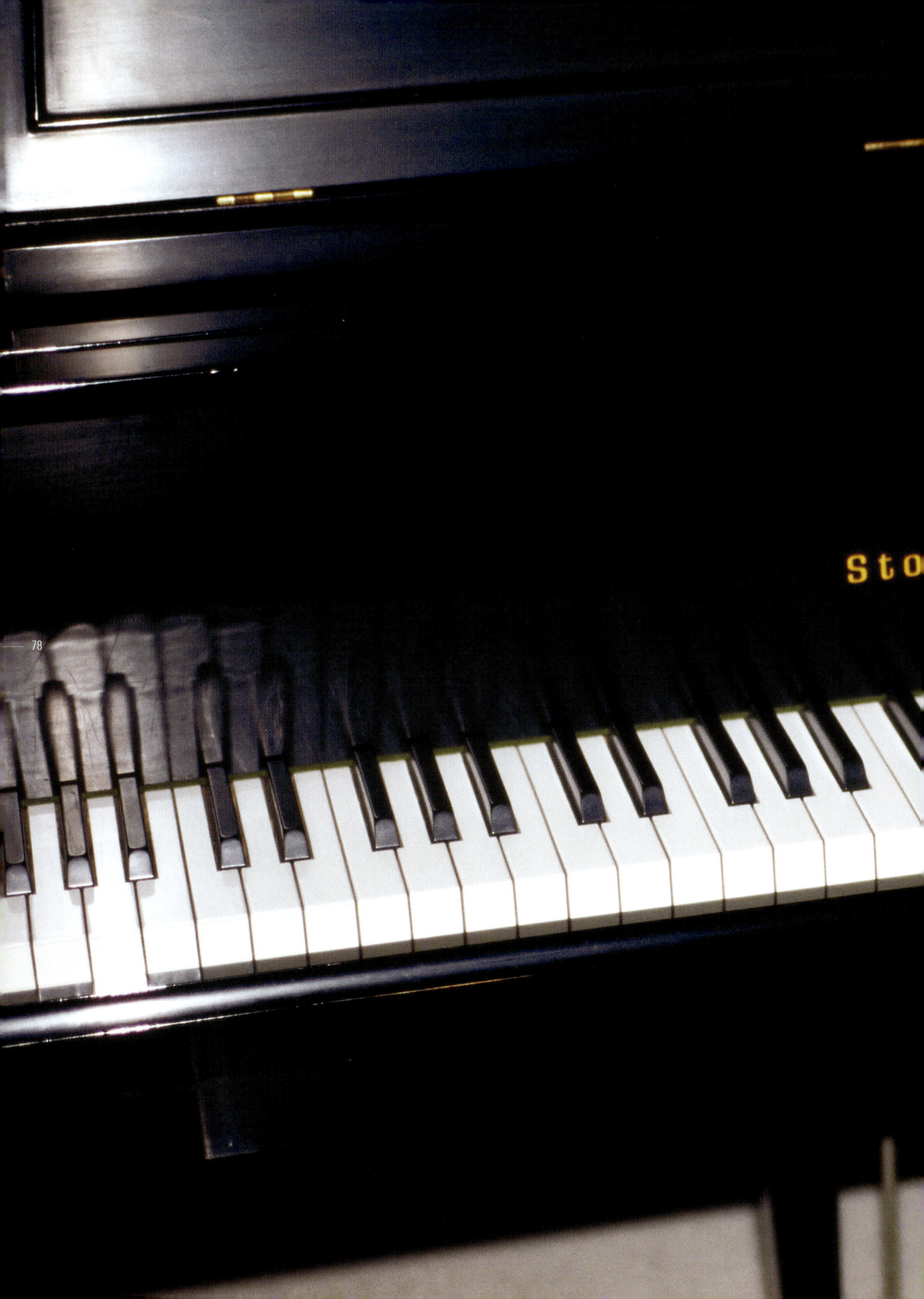
Sto

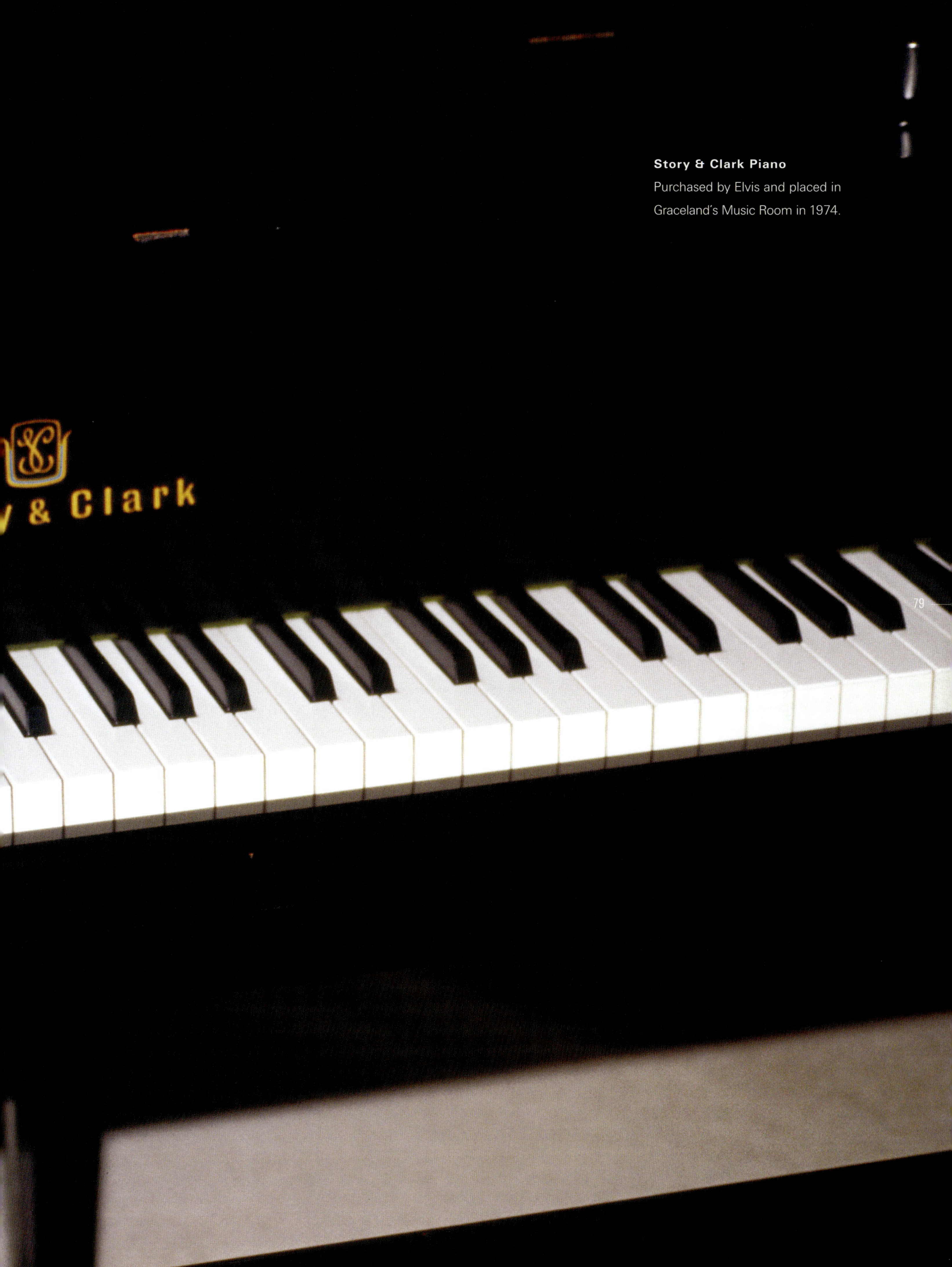

Story & Clark Piano
Purchased by Elvis and placed in Graceland's Music Room in 1974.

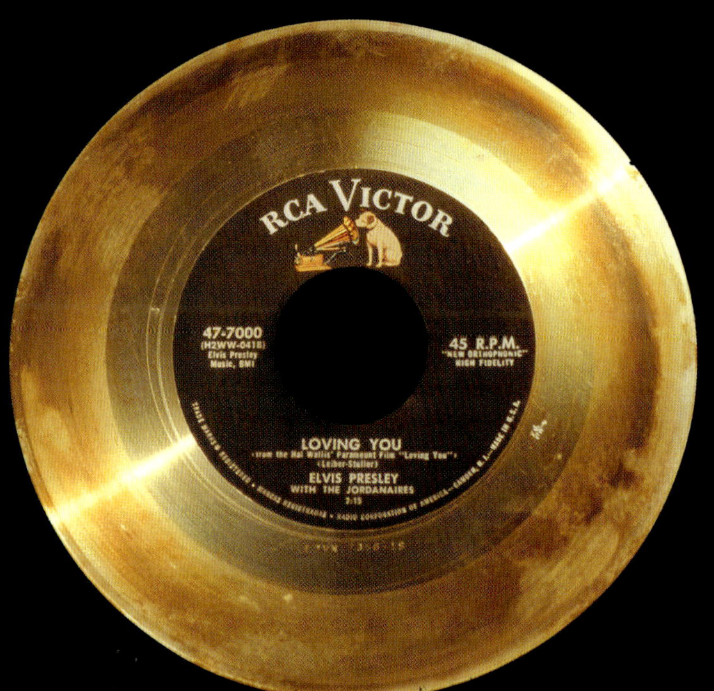

Gold Record

"Loving You" 45.

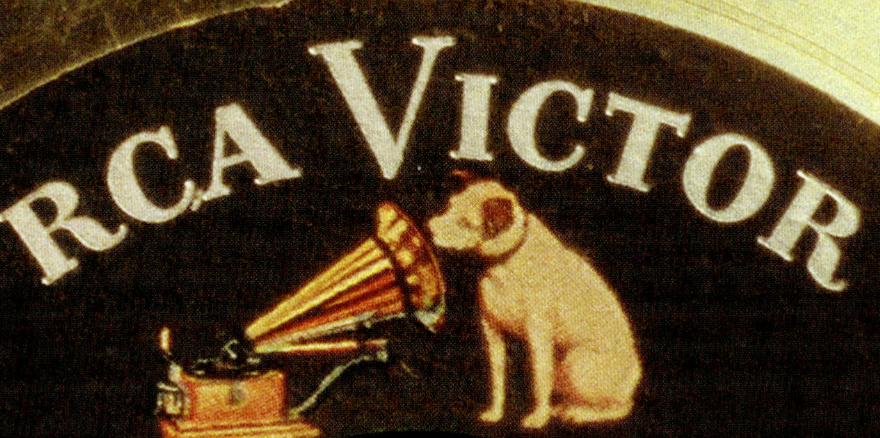
RCA VICTOR
47-7000
(H2WW-0418)
Elvis Presley
Music, BMI
45 R.P.M.
"NEW ORTHOPHONIC"
HIGH FIDELITY
LOVING YOU
(from the Hal Wallis' Paramount Film "Loving You")
(Leiber-Stoller)
ELVIS PRESLEY
WITH THE JORDANAIRES
2:15
TRADE MARKS ® REGISTERED • MARCAS REGISTRADAS • RADIO CORPORATION OF AMERICA—CAMDEN, N.J.—MADE IN U.S.A.

new star popular rmament

practised "picking" on a broom-stick.

A little later he found money enough to buy a cheap instrument and, after more practice and hard work, was able to play tunes. He also sang on street corners to the accompaniment of his guitar.

While still a young boy, he had his first taste of real success when he won a prize in his first public performance at the Tri-State Fair in his home town. And this is where the "show business bug" left its teeth-marks on young Elvis.

Records

Elvis went to high school when his family moved to Memphis, Tennessee and, although his main interest was still with his guitar and his singing, he earned a little extra money by doing odd jobs, including lorry driving.

For the "kicks" and his own amusement, he decided one day to make a private recording—at his own expense. With just this one thought in mind, he walked into the Sun Record Company, Memphis—and, in so doing, walked into stardom!

Sam Phillips, president of Sun Records, heard him sing—and signed him to a contract on the spot. Within a few months, following advice and coaching from Sam, Elvis had his first disc—"That's All Right, Mama"—released on the Sun label. It became an overnight hit—and Elvis has never looked back.

Since then his other discs have caught on with alarming rapidity. Tunes like the aforementioned "Heartbreak Hotel," "Tutti Frutti," "Rag Mop," "I Was The One," "Blue Suede Shoes" and "I Forgot To Remember To Forget" have made him a top recording artist, and an album of words and music to "Elvis Presley Juke Box Favourites" has now been issued in the States.

After graduating from school, Elvis began to make his first personal appearances, and at Shreveport he caused a minor sensation. He won numerous polls, and enlisted the aid of well-known popular c. and w. disc-jockey Bob Neal as his personal manager.

More coast-to-coast personal appearances followed, and as his popularity grew, America's teenagers dubbed him the "King of Western Bop."

Gold disc

Sensation followed sensation! Teenage audiences were drawn to him like metal to a magnet. They screamed louder and louder at each performance, and just one indication

★ ☆ ★ ★ ☆ ★

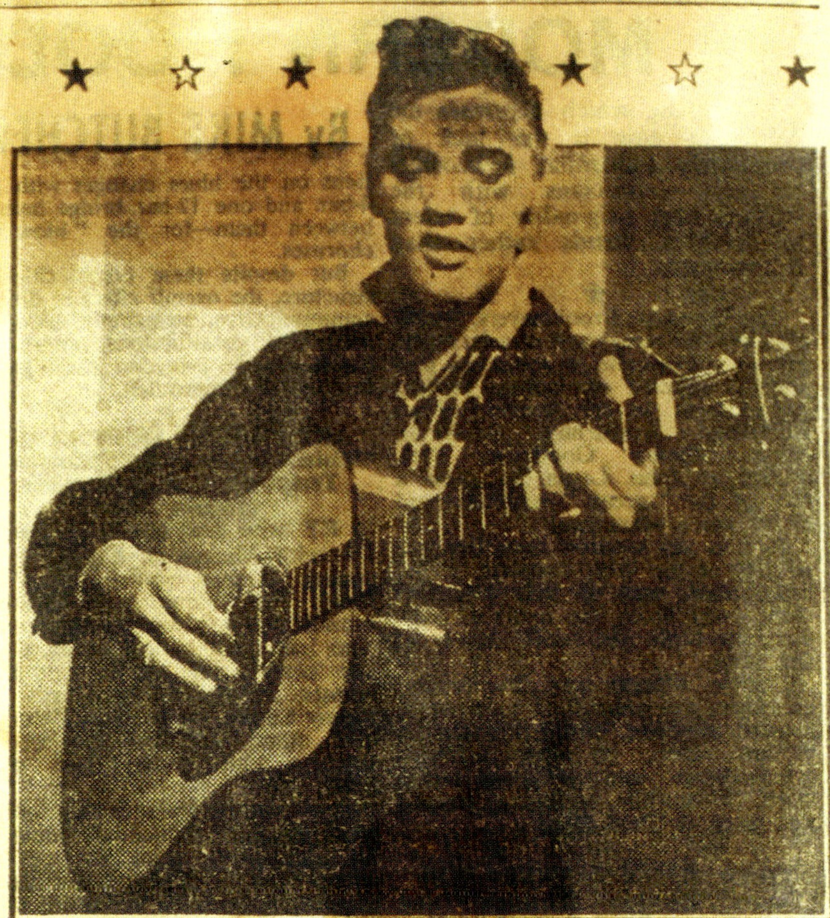

He's 21, 6ft. 2in., with dark, wavy hair and blue eyes. He's a self-taught guitarist. He's the idol of America's teenagers. He's the owner of two Cadillacs. He's the singer whose records are selling in millions in the States. He's—ELVIS PRESLEY.

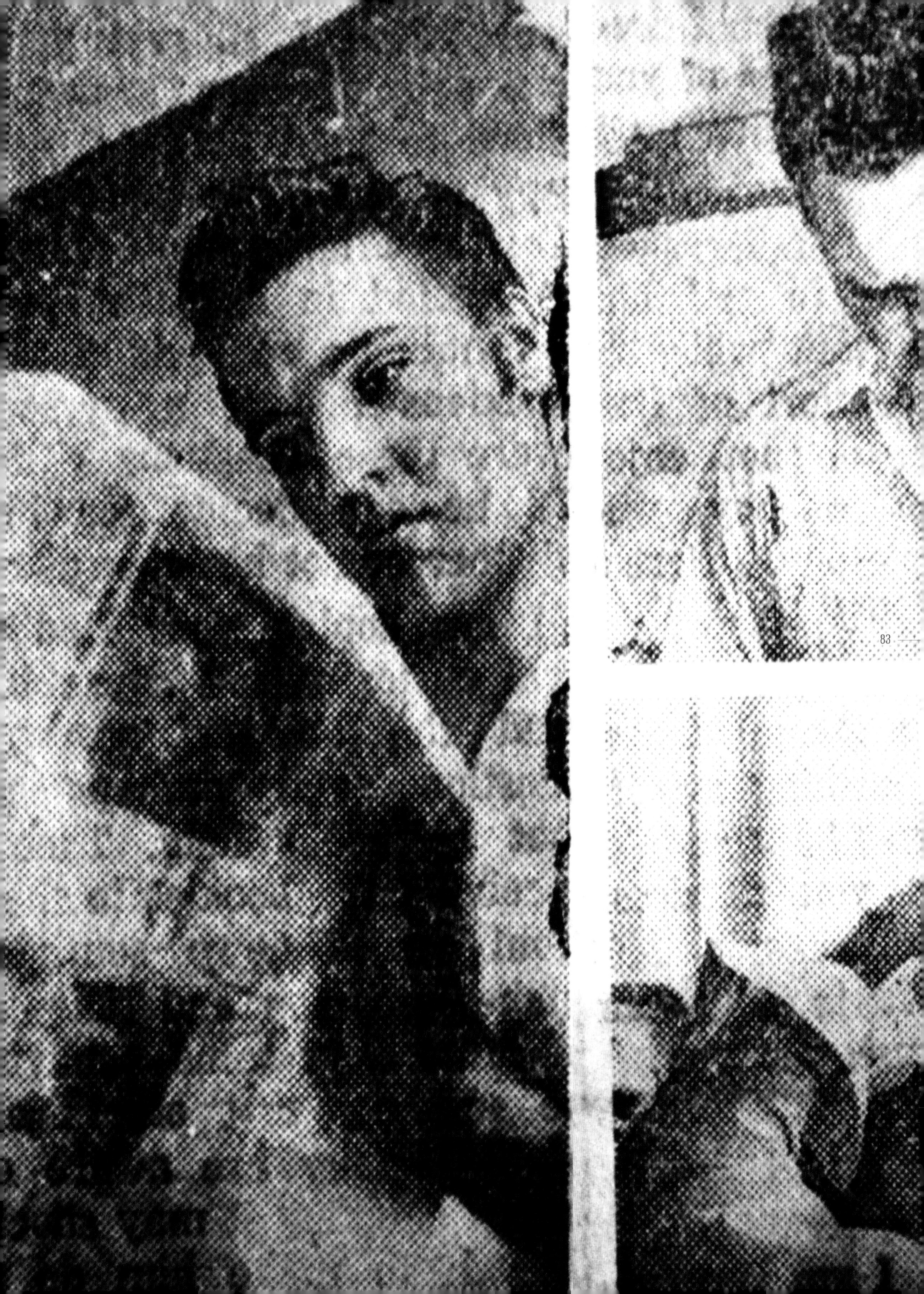

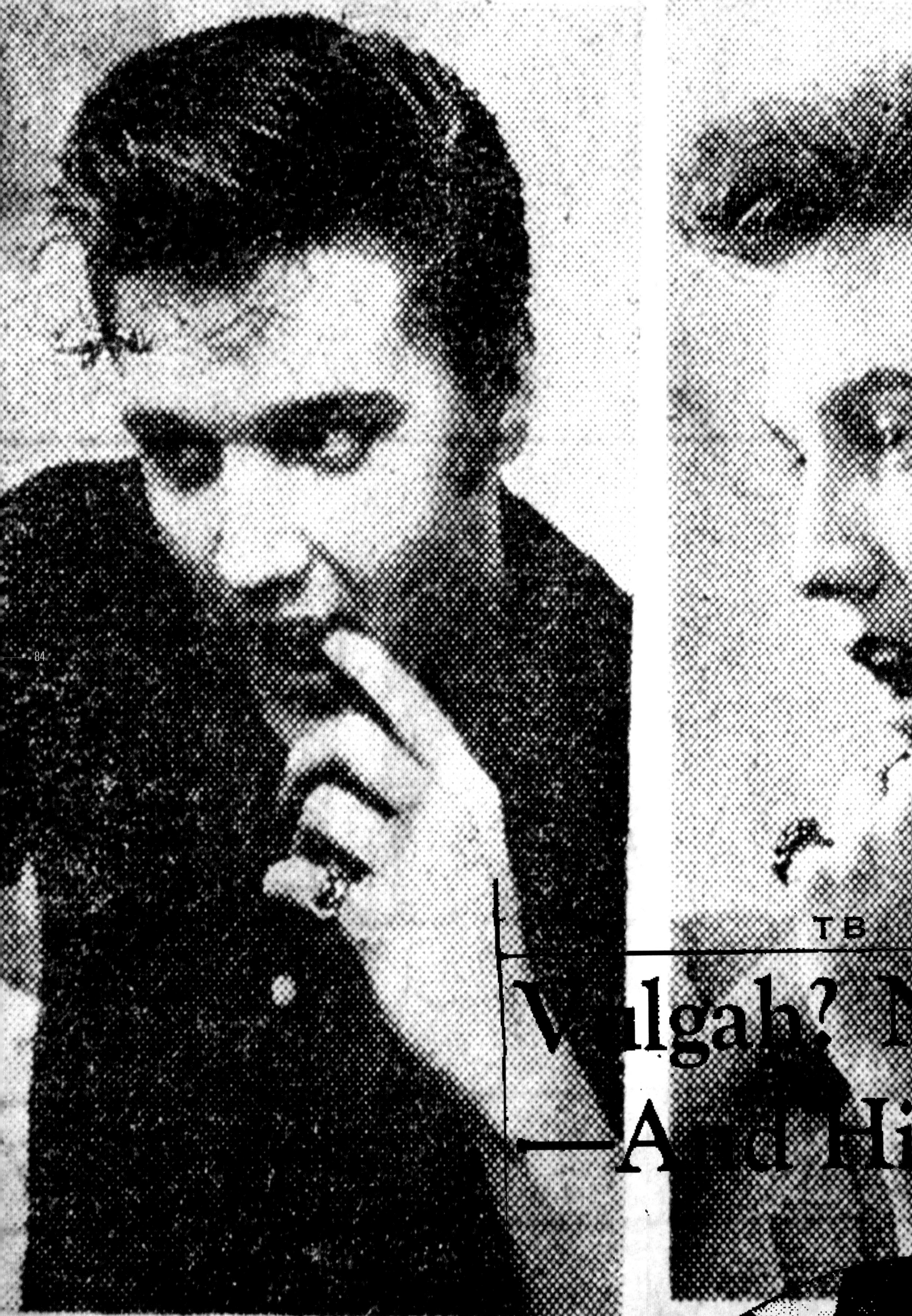
TB

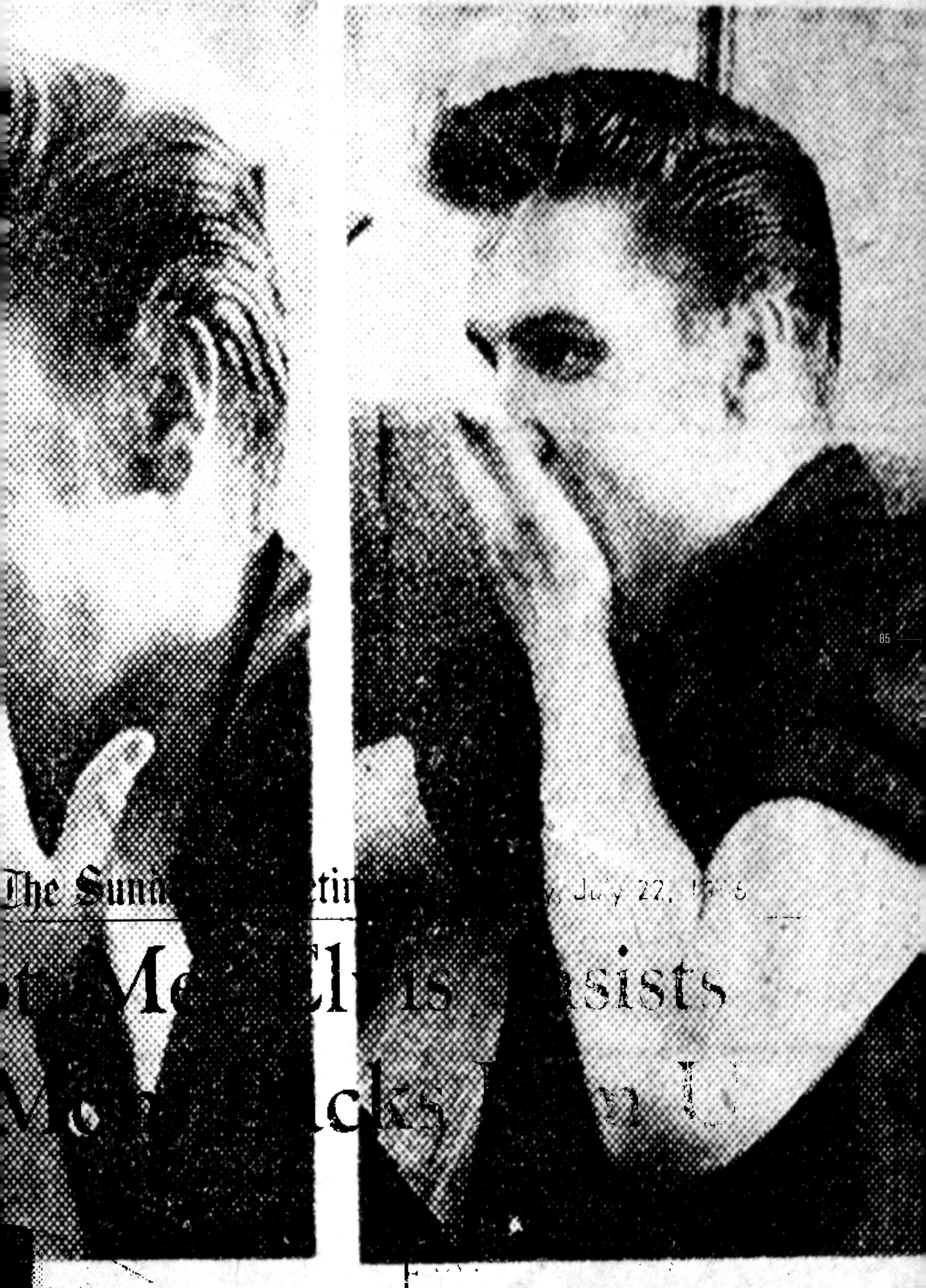
July 22,
Elvis

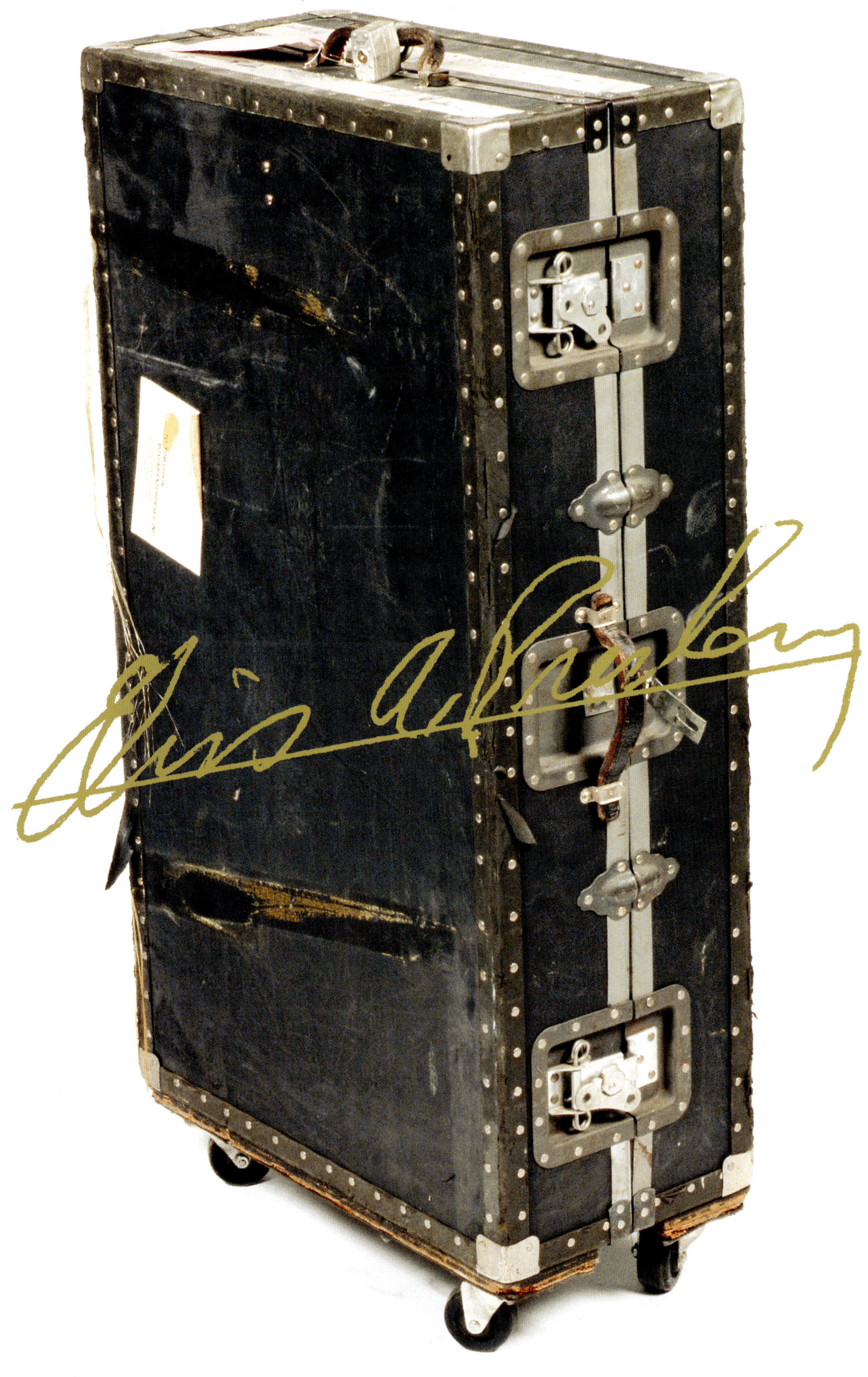

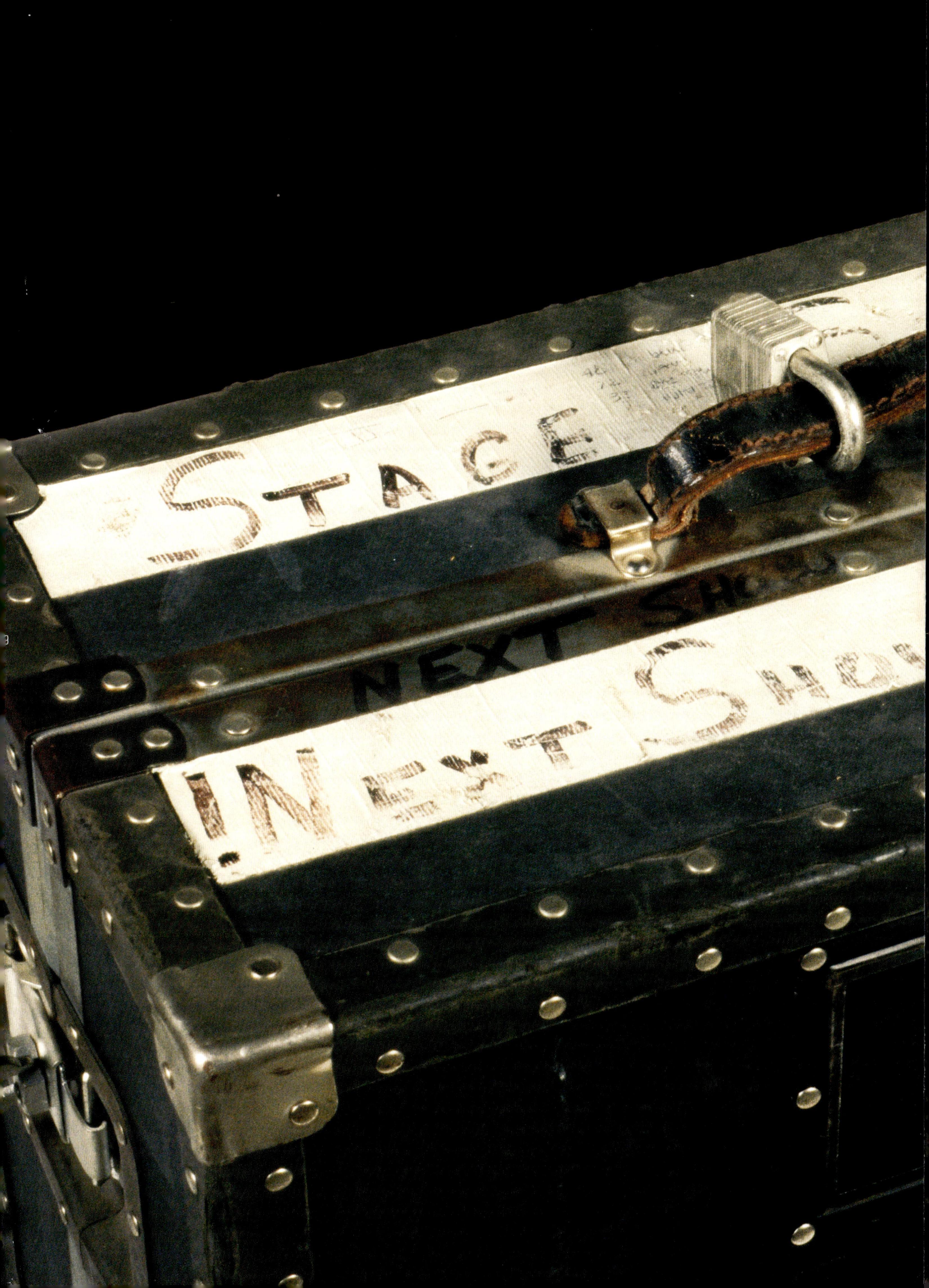
STAGE
NEXT
IN NEXT

Jumpsuit
A close-up of an infamous 1970s-era jumpsuit.

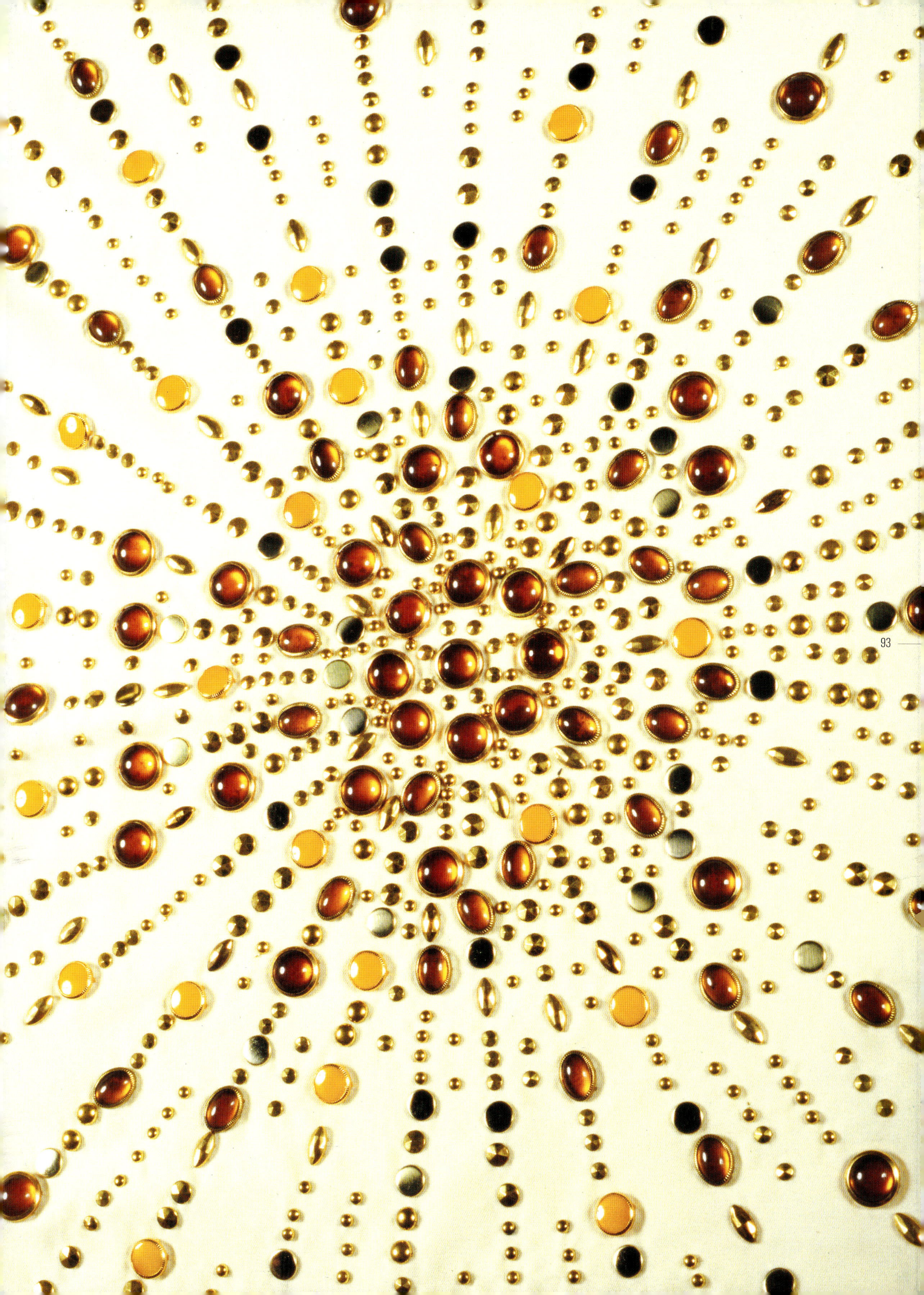

TENNESSEE OPERATOR **LICENSE**

LICENSE NO.	EXPIRATION DATE			HEIGHT	WEIGHT	EYES	HAIR
2571459	01	08	77	600	170	BL	BK

R	S	DATE OF BIRTH			ISSUE DATE			CONDITIONS
W	M	01	08	35	12	17	74	

PRESLEY ELVIS A
3764 HWY 51 S
MEMPHIS TN 38116

Elvis A. Presley

SIGNATURE OF OPERATOR

IBM 879080

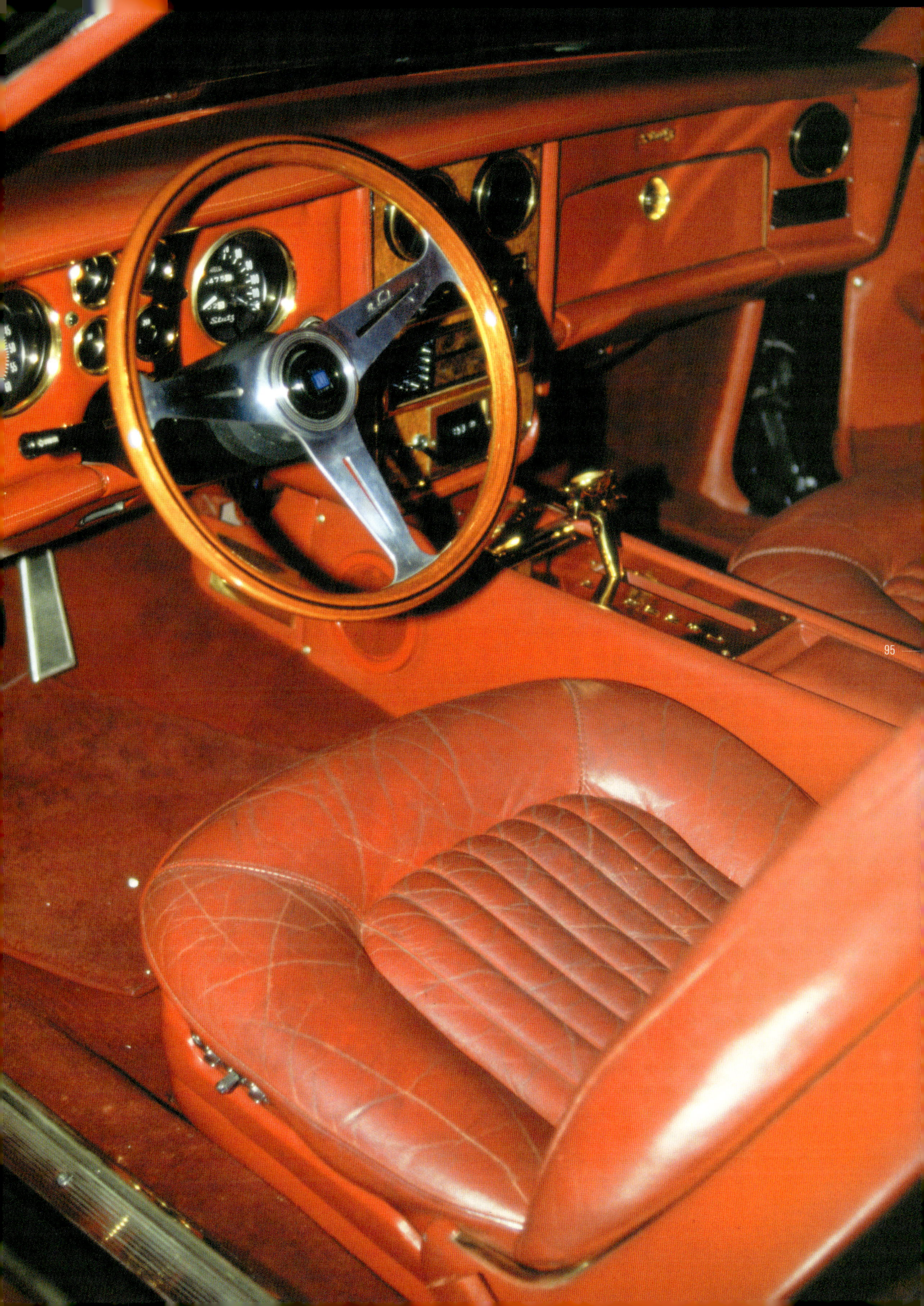

Elvis's Keys
Elvis's car and house keys from his wallet.

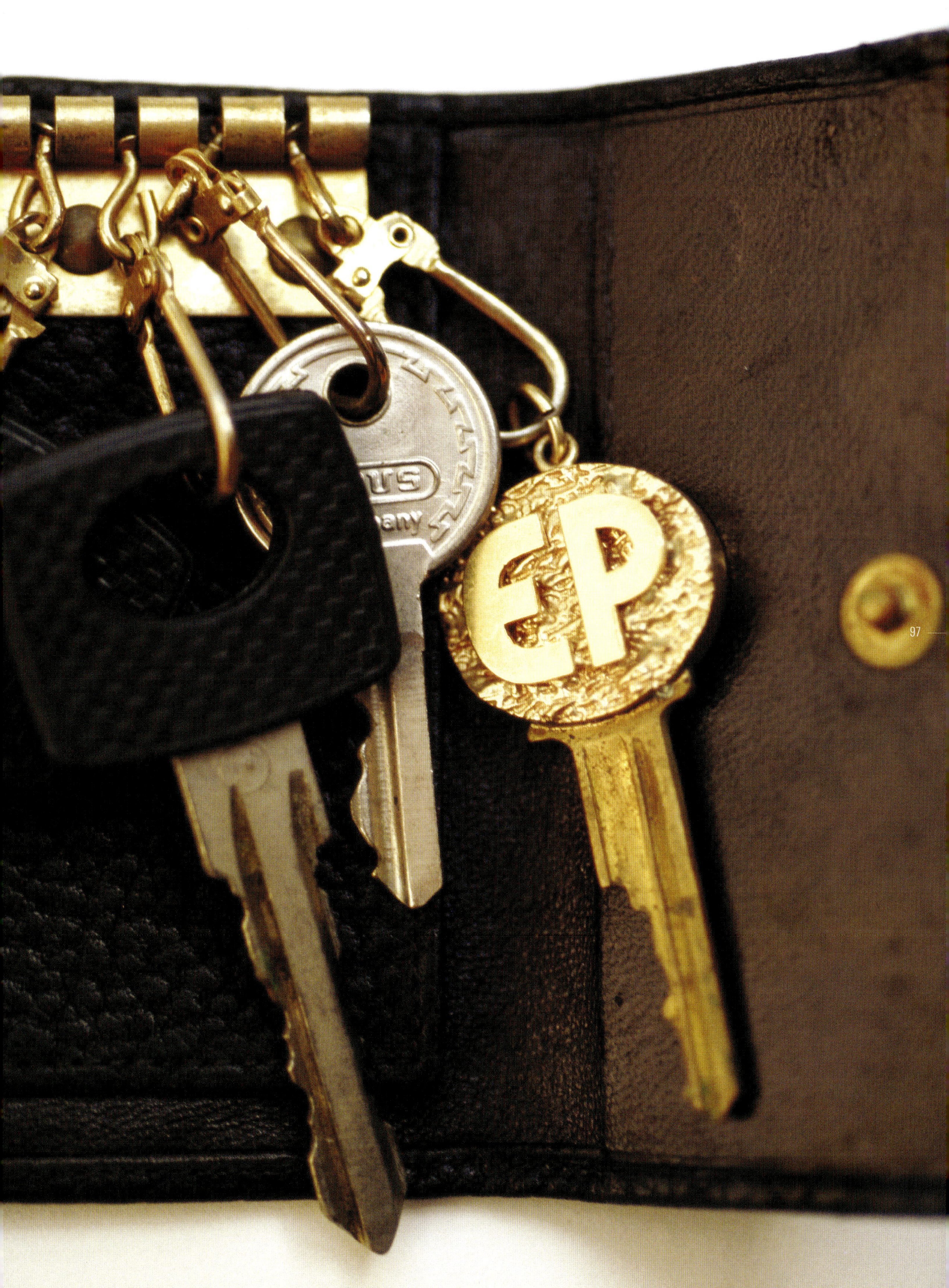
EP

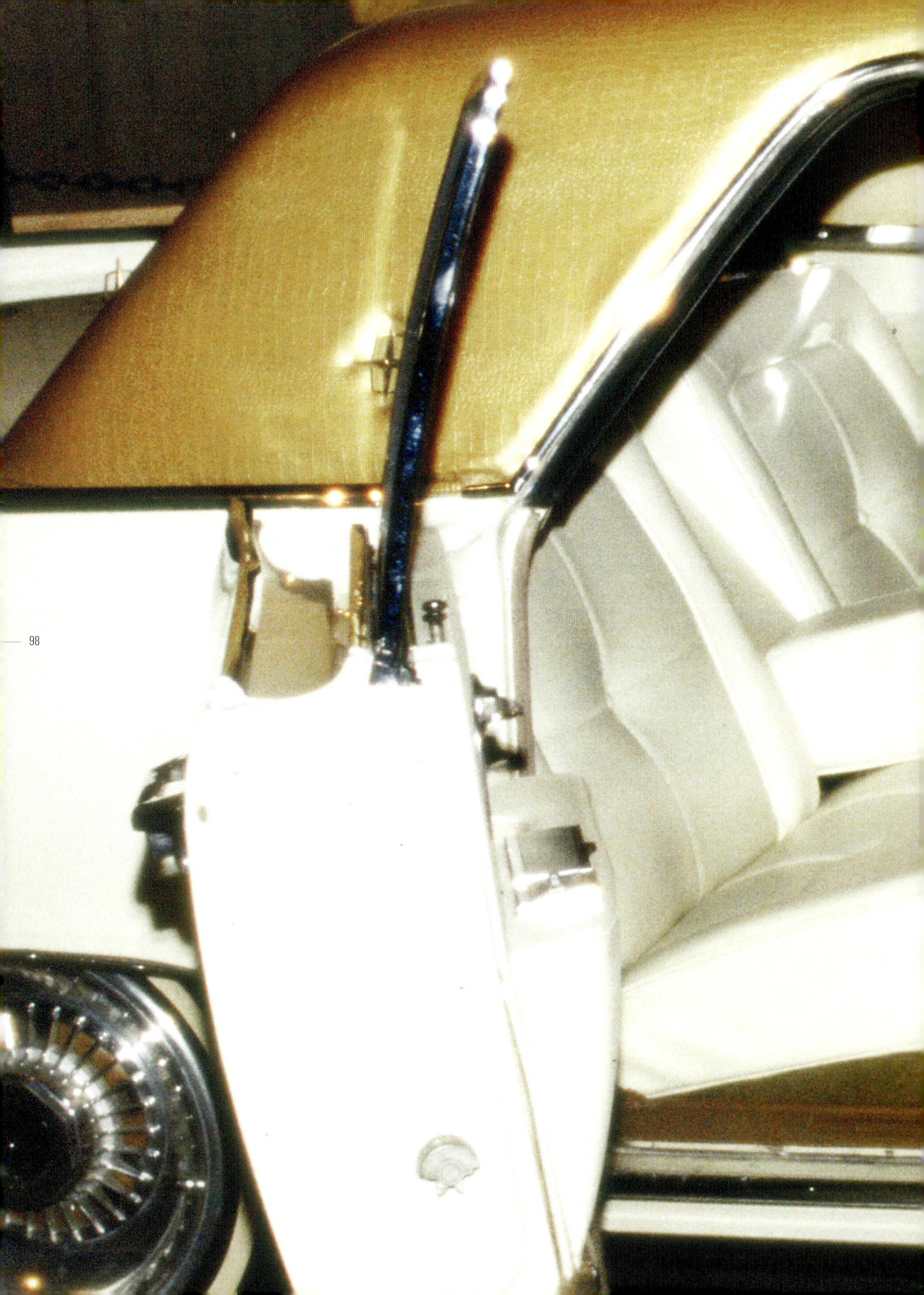

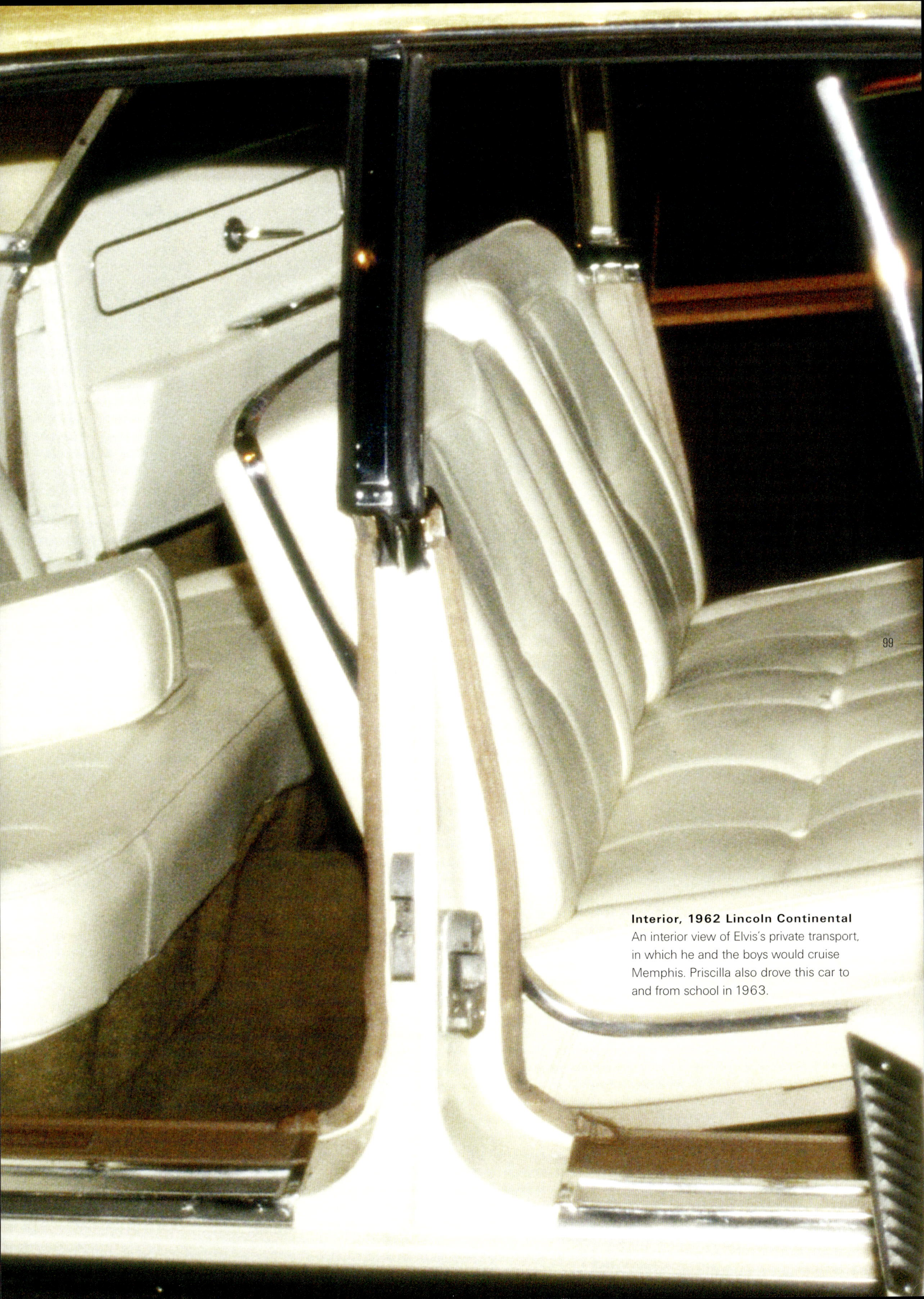

Interior, 1962 Lincoln Continental
An interior view of Elvis's private transport, in which he and the boys would cruise Memphis. Priscilla also drove this car to and from school in 1963.

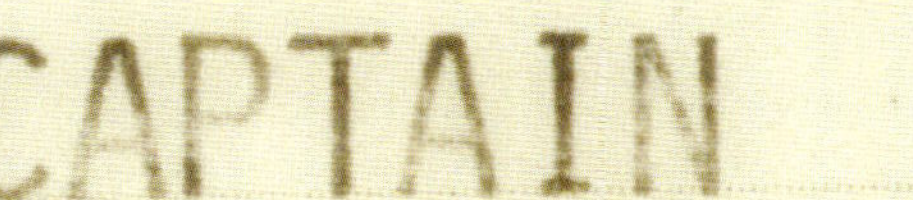
POLICE
TY AND COUNTY OF DENVER
DENVER POLICE
CAPTAIN
RANK
ELVIS PRESLEY
NAME
Arthur G. Dill
CHIEF OF POLICE - DENVER, COLORADO

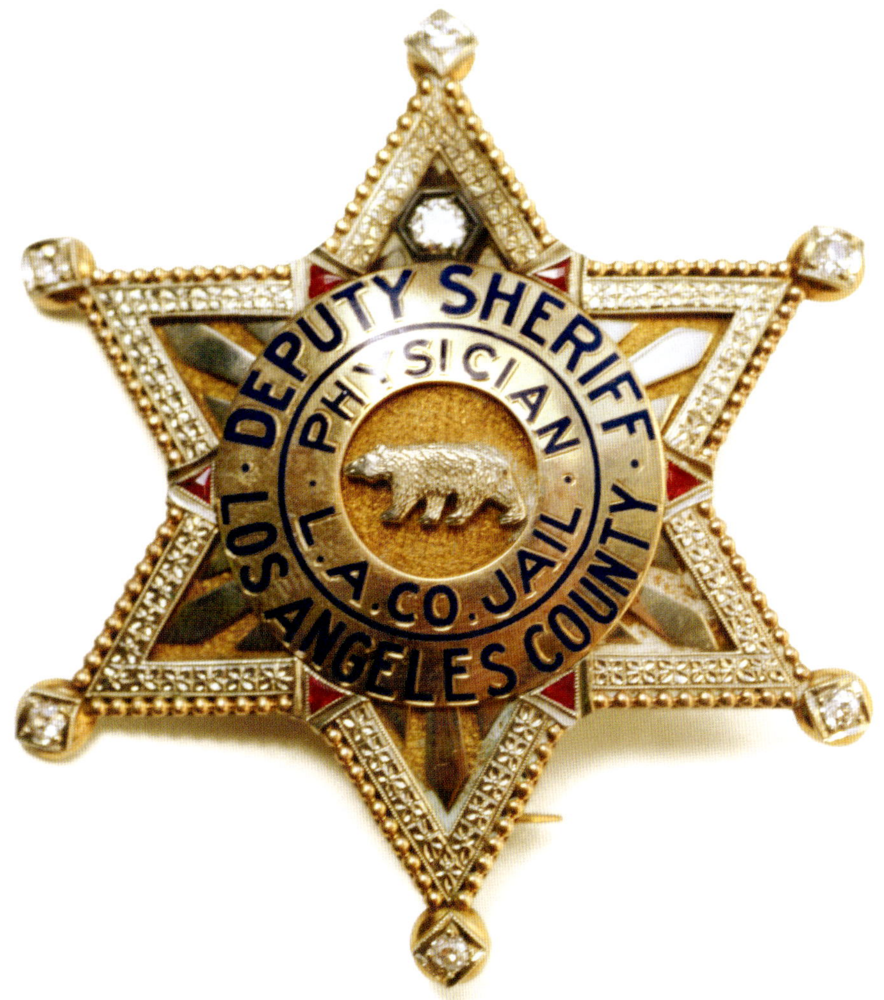

Diamond-Studded Police Badge
A friend on the Denver police force gave Elvis this badge.

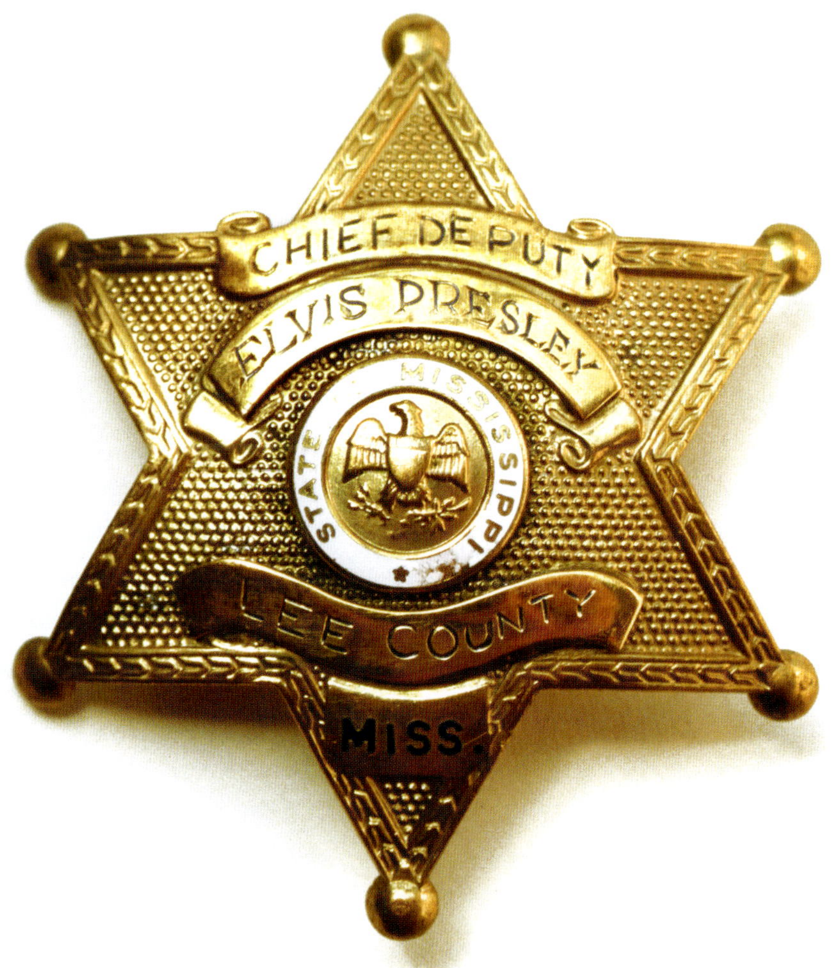

Object Of Authority
The pairing of Elvis's Colt .45 semiautomatic gun with his federal narcotics badge establishes the paradox between Elvis's rebel reputation and his lifelong obsession with authority.

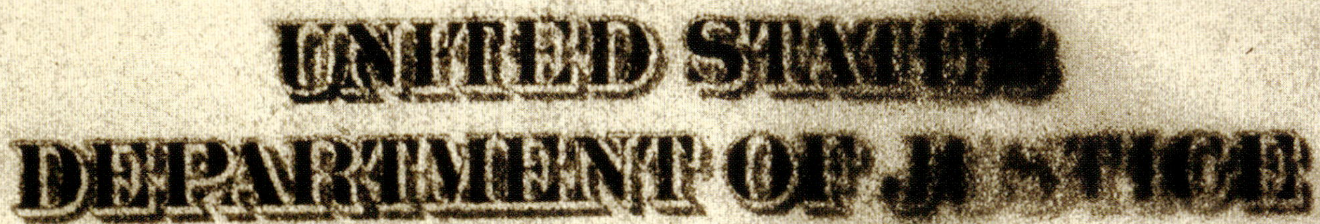

THIS IS TO CERTIFY THAT

ELVIS PRESLEY

WHOSE SIGNATURE AND PHOTOGRAPH APPEAR BELOW

IS DULY APPOINTED AS

SPECIAL ASSISTANT

IN

BUREAU OF NARCOTICS AND

DANGEROUS DRUGS

AND IS AUTHORIZE

BUREAU TO PERFO

DUTIES CONSISTENT

SPECIAL ADVISORY

Elvis A. Presley

SIGNATURE

BUREAU DIRECTOR

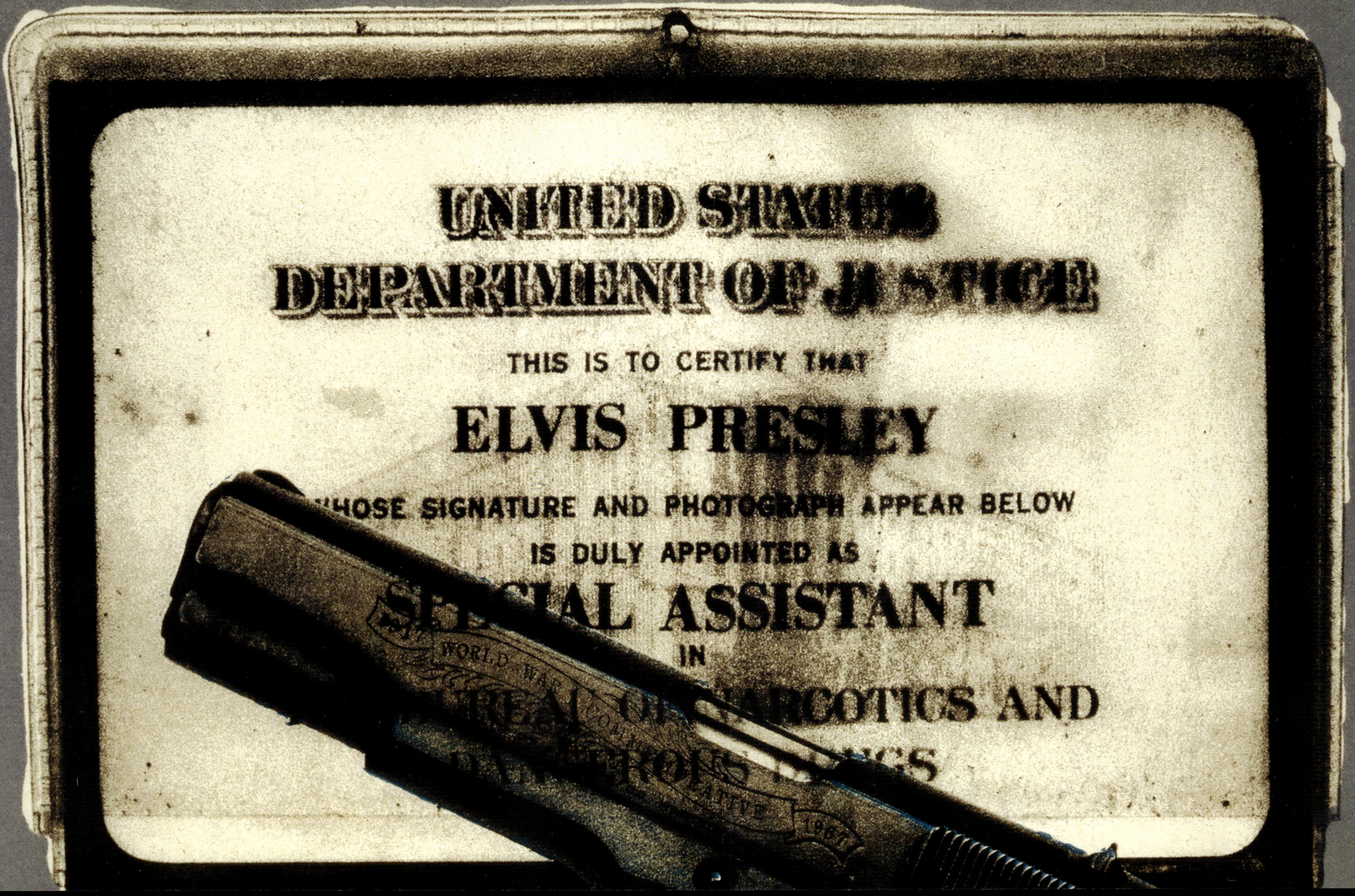

THIS IS TO CERTIFY THAT
ELVIS PRESLEY
IS DULY APPOINTED AS
IN

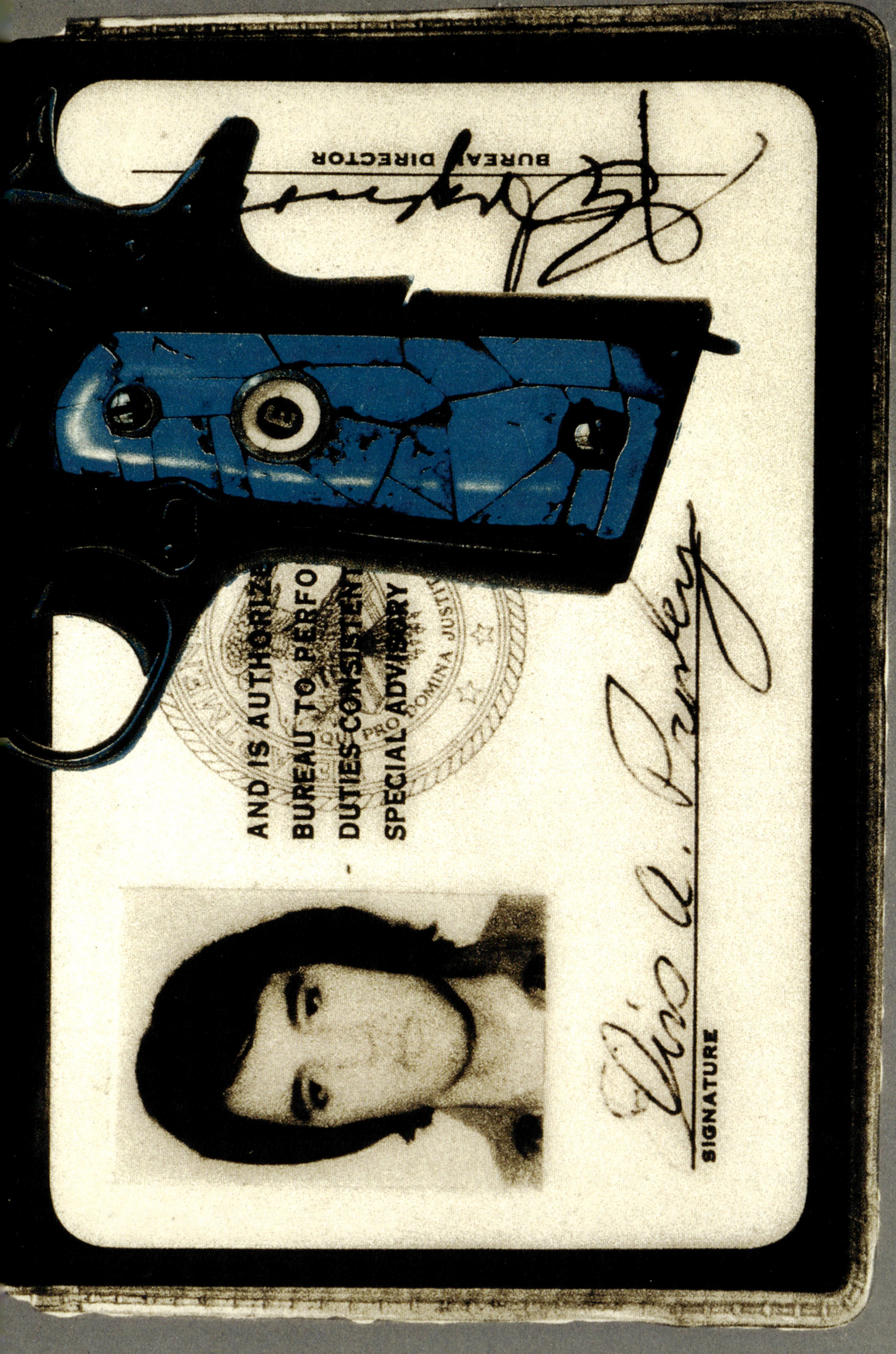

BUREAU DIRECTOR

AND IS AUTHORIZE
BUREAU TO PERFO
DUTIES CONSISTENT
SPECIAL ADVISORY

SIGNATURE

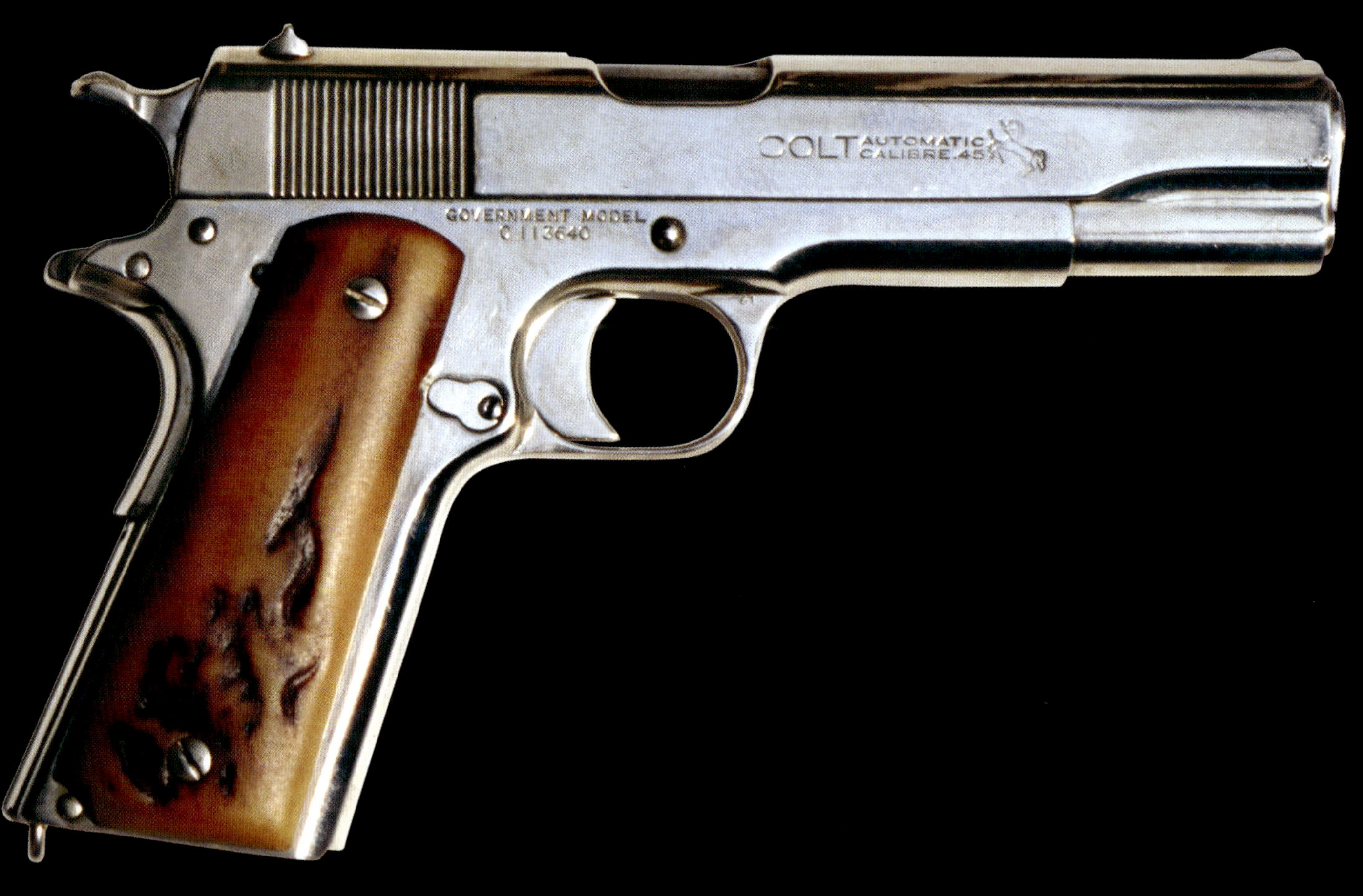
COLT AUTOMATIC CALIBRE .45
GOVERNMENT MODEL
C 113640

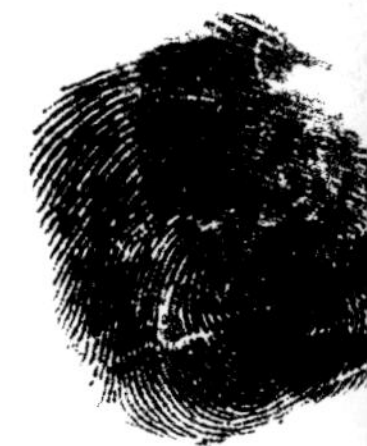

Colt Pistol With Ingrained Wood Handle
One of several colt pistols that Elvis owned.

Tupelo Fireplace
Elvis's birthplace in Tupelo. This home is where Elvis was born on January 8, 1935, to Gladys and Vernon Presley.

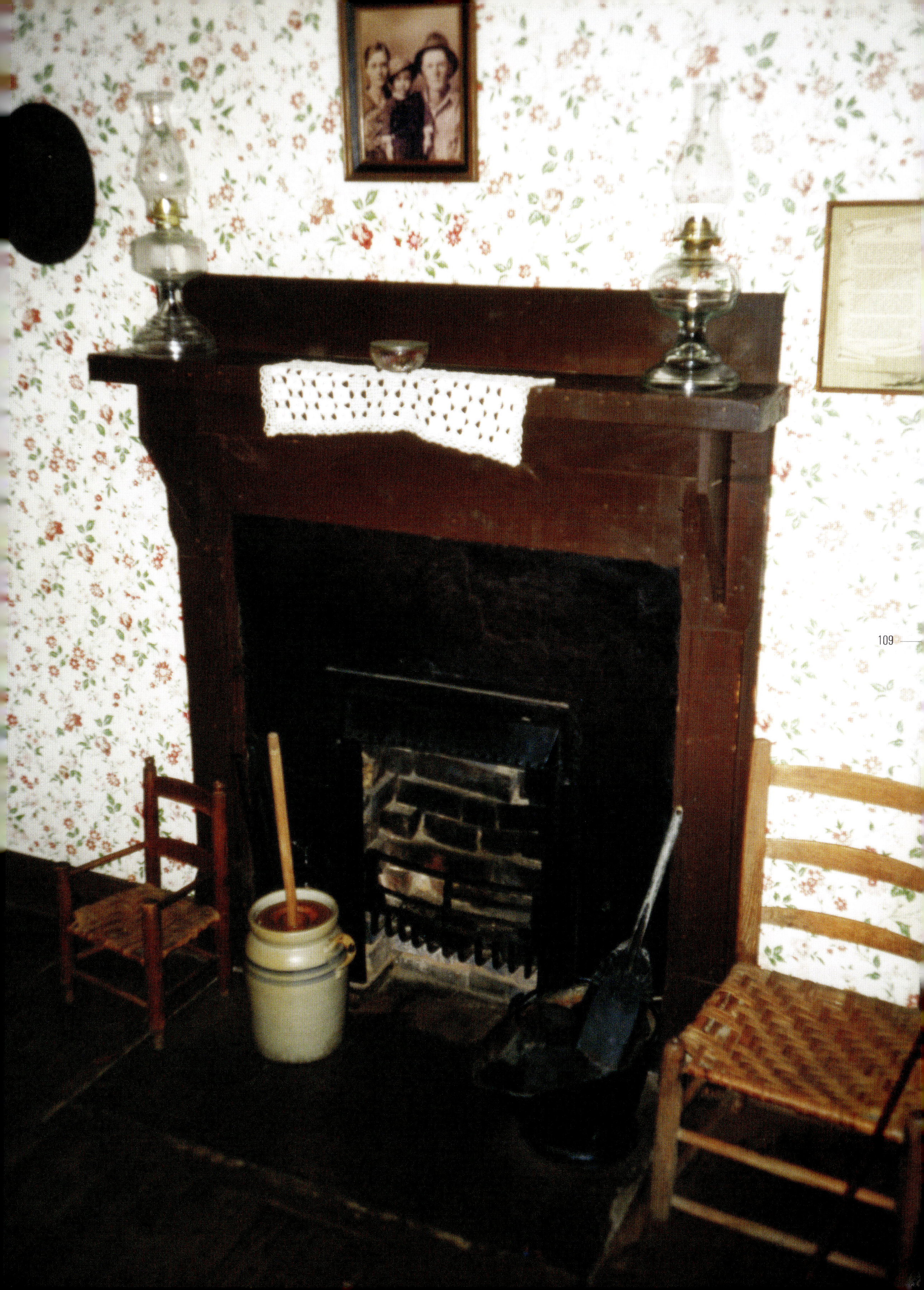

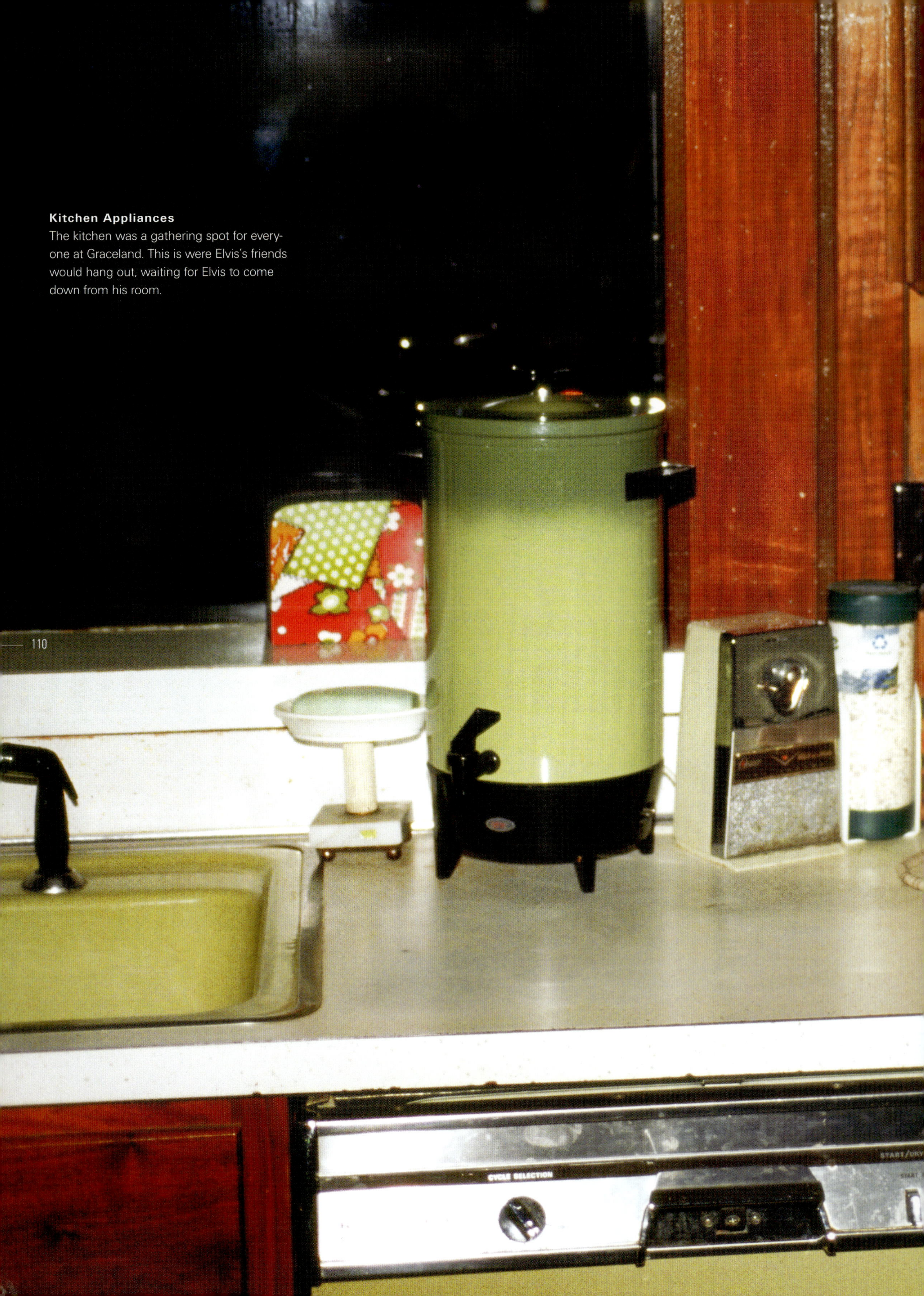

Kitchen Appliances

The kitchen was a gathering spot for everyone at Graceland. This is were Elvis's friends would hang out, waiting for Elvis to come down from his room.

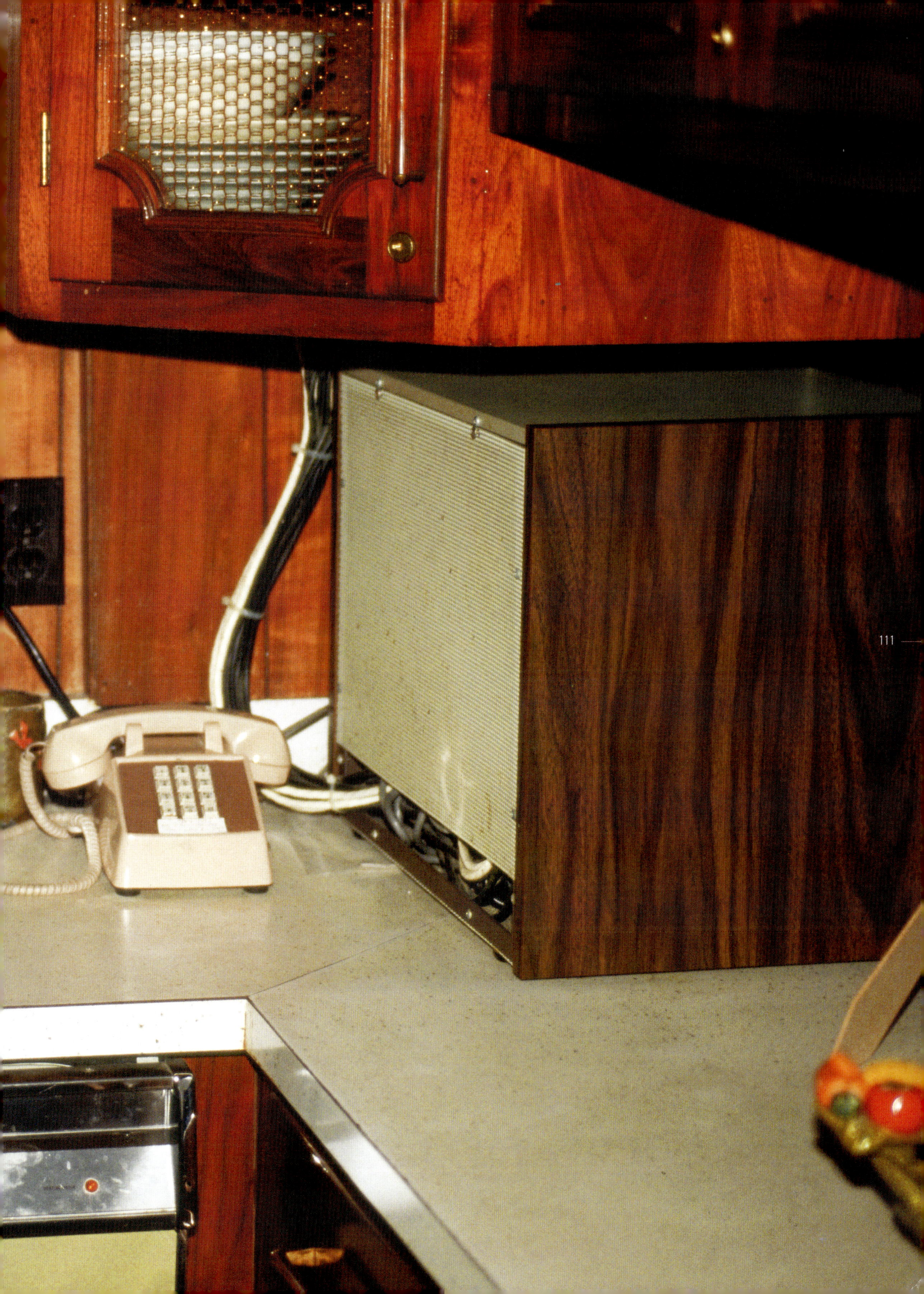

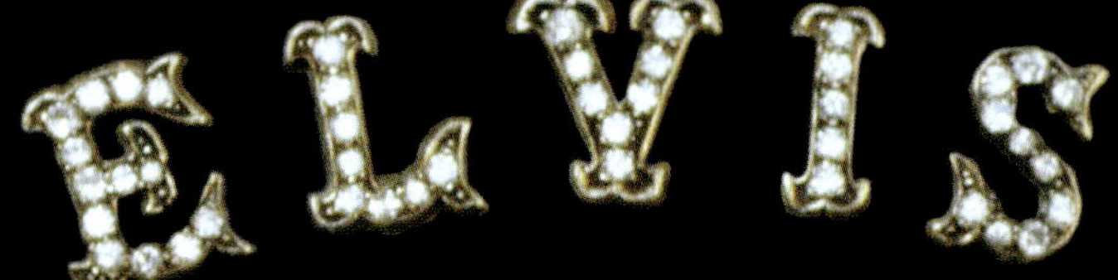
ELVIS

Elvis May Move Into $100,000 Mansion in Whitehaven

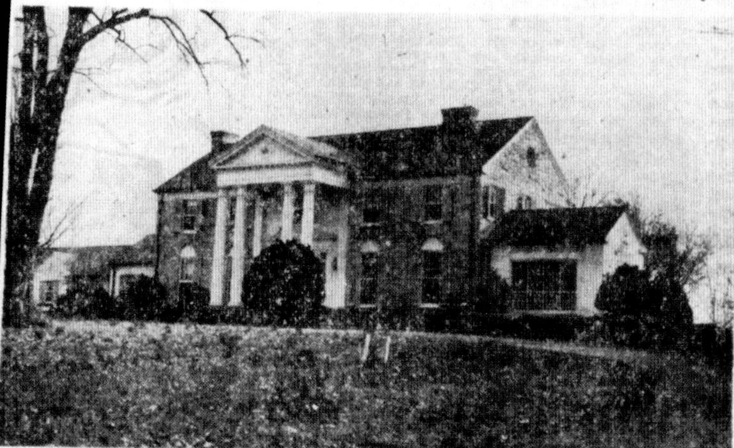

ELVIS HOUSE? Maybe. Graceland, the lovely Whitehaven estate placed on the market by Mrs. Ruth Brown Moore, was much admired by Memphis' famous singing star and his parents, Mr. and Mrs. Vernon Presley, this week. "I want some room to stretch out in," said Elvis. Graceland has it, in a big house and nearly 14 surrounding acres.

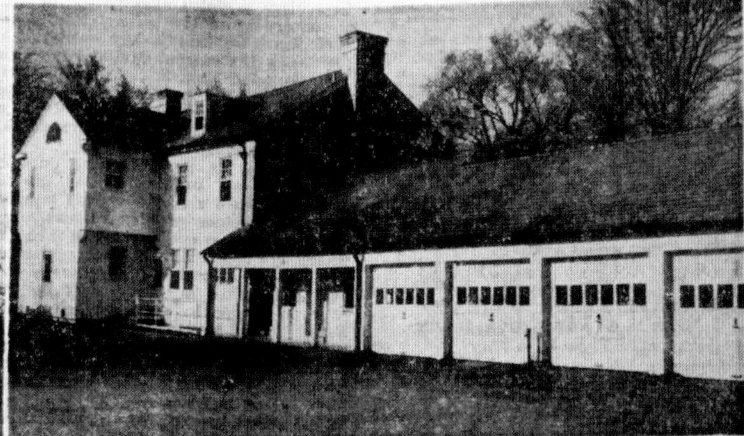

—Press-Scimitar Staff Photos

NOTHING BUT GARAGES in one long wing, shown from the back. One for the Mark II Continental, two, three and four for the Cadillacs, and nowhere for the Messerschmidt and the motorcycle. Stairway at left leads to the basement, where there is a big den and a playroom.

THRU THESE PORTALS may pass one of the nation's most famous young men, if Elvis buys Graceland. Hewn stone walls, arched over the windows, and the towering pillars of the entrance make it one of Shelby County's most impressive homes.

* * *

Singer Is Interested in Purchasing Graceland

Elvis Presley and his parents, Mr. and Mrs. Vernon Presley, are interested in buying Graceland, a Southern Colonial mansion at Whitehaven.

"This is going to be a lot nicer than Red Skelton's house when I get it like I want it," Elvis said enthusiastically after he went thru the house for the first time Tuesday.

Skelton's home is a fabulous hilltop house with a mile and a half drive from the gate and garages for his 11 cars. It is an outstanding showplace of Hollywood. Graceland has a four-car garage—barely big enough to house all of Presley's cars in Memphis. (He has another one on the West Coast.)

'Just the Thing'

Elvis' parents were shown the place last Saturday, soon after they arrived in Memphis from Hollywood, by Mrs. Virginia Grant of Virginia Grant Realty Co. Elvis arrived Monday night and went to see it the next day. He agreed with them that it was "just the thing."

However, no papers have been signed. "We've found a house that we like very much, and we will buy it if we can come to terms," said Elvis' father.

Graceland is reported to be priced at about $100,000.

If a deal is made, the Presleys would move in as soon as possible, probably around April 15, it was learned.

The Presleys were trying to keep their plans secret, but news about Elvis leaks fast.

Mrs. Grant had showed them one other property previously.

The Owner

Owner of Graceland is Mrs. Ruth Brown Moore, who has bought and moved into another home at 2405 Union Extended. Hugh Bosworth of Bosworth, Inc., is listing agent.

A complete redecoration of the house is planned by the Presleys, if they buy the house. It will be carpeted wall-to-wall, even in the basement, which contains a big wood-paneled den and a playroom, with two fireplaces.

The 13¾ acres offered with the house would be used largely for horseback riding, etc. The Presleys would build a swimming pool and make other outdoor improvements.

The grounds would be enclosed with a chain-link fence to insure privacy that was lacking in the smaller property occupied by the Presleys at 1034 Audubon Drive.

Taken in Trade

The house on Audubon would be taken in trade by Mrs. Moore and put on the market. Originally costing about $35,000, it has had many expensive improvements, including an addition, a swimming pool, wood paneling thruout, and inclosure decorated with musical notes.

An indication of the swiftness with which the family became interested in the larger house is that their present property is thickly dotted with new trees planted just before the recent trip to California.

Graceland, the two-story stone residence of Southern Colonial architecture, featuring a tall, stone-pillared portico on the front, is both spacious and charming.

What It Includes

It includes an entrance stair-hall, living room, dining room and parlor across the front that can be opened for entertaining into an area 75 feet long. A big kitchen, pantry, butler's pantry, utility room, one bedroom and a bath and a half are on the ground floor. Upstairs are four bedrooms and three baths.

The property is beautifully wooded and planted.

Closest neighbor will be Graceland Christian Church, which recently received 4½ acres of the original property as a gift from Mrs. Moore. The rest of the famous Hereford cattle farm has been developed into Graceland Subdivision and Whitehaven Plaza Shopping Center.

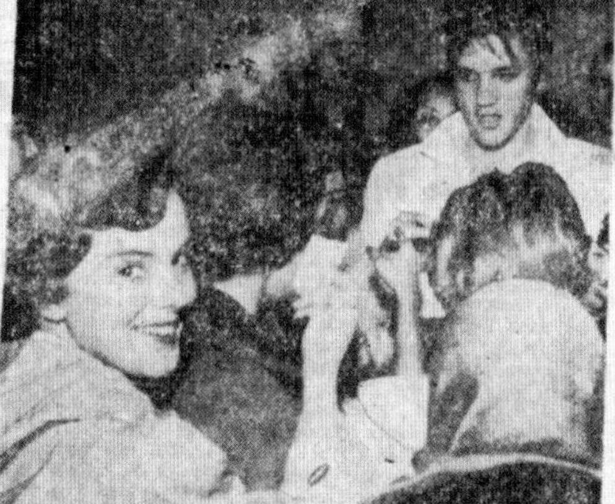

—Press-Scimitar Staff Photo

WHEREVER ELVIS GOES, GIRLS FLOCK—And the usual happened when Elvis Presley parked his Continental Mark II on the lot across from Hotel Chisca last night. Girls flocked around for autographs. So did boys, but in this picture, some of the boys look a bit disconsolate in the background.

Elvis Growing A Mustache!

It's a little thing—but it's big news.

Elvis is growing a mustache! Pictures made of Elvis last night clearly show the darkish smudge on his upper lip. (Picture on Page 1.) "Mustache" pictures were made by The Press-Scimitar as long ago as last Monday but the mustache failed to show in the prints then.

Whether he's growing it for his next movie or just for fun, or to improve his looks couldn't be learned. All Elvis would say is that it is the start on a mustache. He started letting it grow on his long train trip last week end.

He still has the sideburns and the dark brown hair that won't stay put.

Elvis tooled his 1956 Continental Mark II $11,575 auto into the parking lot across from Hotel Chisca at 10:30 last night, just as the Traffic Safety banquet was breaking up.

A typical Elvis jam session resulted, with so many teen-agers about that the car couldn't be moved for awhile.

Commissioner and Mrs. Stanley Dillard and Capt. and Mrs. Joe Griffin (he is a school safety officer) came out of the safety banquet and watched the scene with amazement. Mrs. Dillard and Mrs. Griffin wanted to get closer. Soon Commissioner Dillard was shaking hands with Elvis, and Mrs. Dillard said she got him into it, Stanley said he admires Presley.

Elvis will leave Wednesday for Chicago to open a 10-day road trip.

So there won't be any jam scenes with teen-agers until he returns. And the mustache may be a lot more noticeable by the time he gets back.

Portrait
This portrait was done while Elvis was on leave from the Army in 1958. It is an actual photograph done over with oil paint. It shows Elvis's true hair color of Blonde.

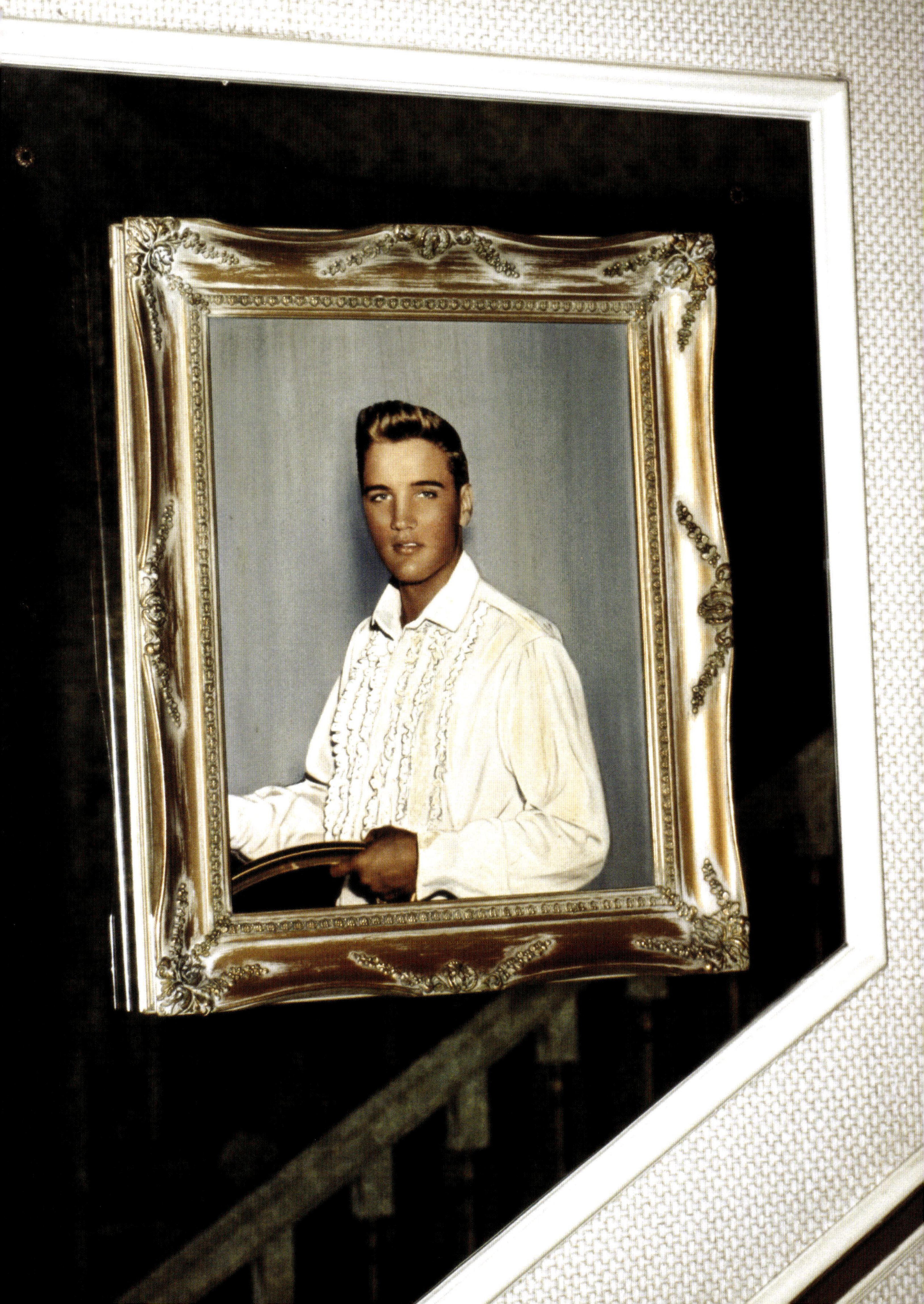

The first edition of **Elvis: The Personal Archives** is published by

Channel Photographics LLC
116 East 16th Street, 12th Floor, New York, NY 10003
Phone: 212-254-5240
Fax: 212-254-5246
Email: info@channelphotographics.com
www.channelphotographics.com

Please contact Jeff Scott at:
Jeff Scott Studio
660 Preston Forest Ctr. #399, Dallas, TX. 75230

Phone: 214-908-0295
Email: jeff@jeffscottstudio.com
www.jeffscottstudio.com

Distributed by SCB DISTRIBUTORS
15608 South New Century Drive, Gardena, CA 90248
Phone: 310-532-9400
Fax: 310-532-7001

Printed in China by Global PSD
First edition 2005
ISBN: 0-9766708-2-8

Designers: Jim Foley, Shelly Fletchall, Loudthought
www.loudthought.biz

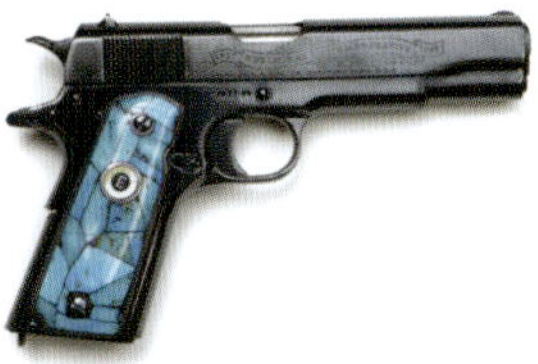

ACKNOWLEDGEMENTS

I would like to thank Jim Foley, who helped me design this book with stamina and patience. Also; James Crump and Gordon Goff, Kelly Hill, Debbie Johnson, Carol Butler, Jack Soden, Angie Marchese, Sheila James, Susan Sherwood, Danny Hiltenbrand, Jay Etkin, E.A. Carmean, Jr., Vicky Boyd, Craig and Jennifer Todd, John Smith, Elise and Scott, Dana Foley, Katherine Brimberry, Mark Smith, Robert Brown, Don Messec, Marian Fried, Steve Stinehour, Jason Siegal, Kristy Stubbs, Myers and Londa, Matt Louis, Lauren and Chris, Tracy, Julie, Hal and Bernard Lansky, Mark and Kelly Hood, Charlie Wylie, Charles McGarry, Jack Mathews, Jeff West, my Parents and Elvis Presley.

DESIGN: JEFF SCOTT & JIM FOLEY

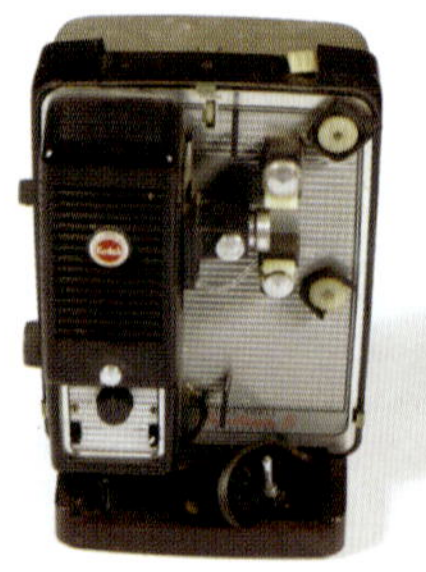

JEFF SCOTT

Jeff Scott is an artist known for his dramatic imagery of America's historic and cultural landscape. He has exhibited widely in the United States, and his work is in the permanent collections of the Dallas Museum of Art and the Smithsonian Institution, as well as Elvis Presley Enterprises, Disneyland, Polo Ralph Lauren, and the National Trust for Historic Preservation. Portions of his series based on Elvis's personal archives were exhibited recently at the Andy Warhol Museum, Pittsburgh.

E.A. CARMEAN, JR.

E.A. Carmean, Jr. is a former curator of twentieth-century art at The National Gallery of Art, Washington, DC and the former director of the Modern Art Museum of Fort Worth. A noted art historian, Carmean, Jr. is the author of numerous books and catalogues in the visual arts including, *Picasso: The Saltimbanques* (1980); *L'Atelier de Jackson Pollock* (1991); *Coming to Light: Avery, Gottlieb, Rothko — Provincetown Summers,* 1957-1961 (2003); *Helen Frankenthaler: A Painting Retrospective* (1989); *David Smith* (1982), *Great Decade of American Abstraction: Modernist Art, 1960 to 1970* (1983); and *Bellows: The Boxing Pictures* (1982).

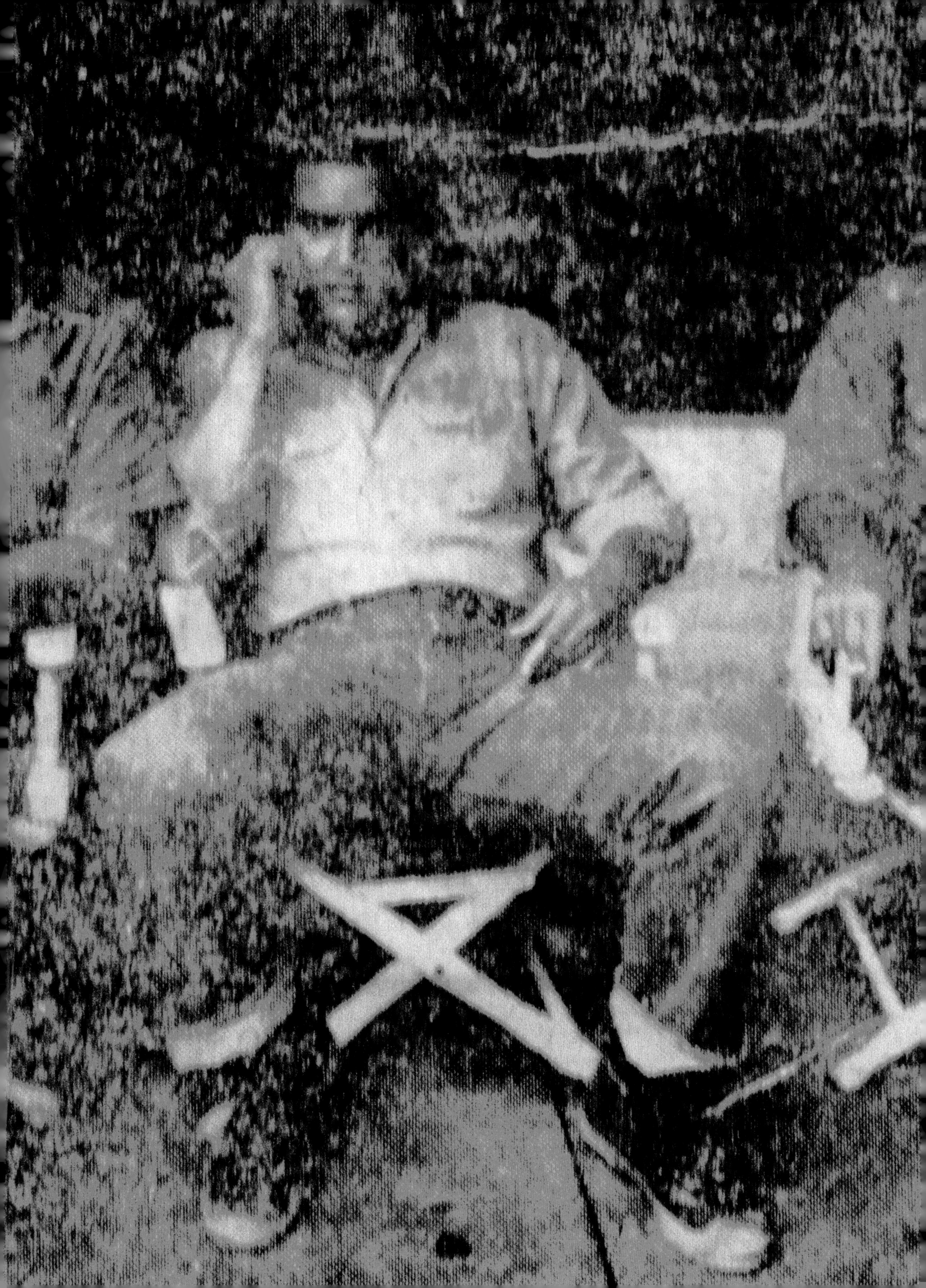

Elvis the Pelvis Way to Fame

City Incident Incidental

Indianapolis was a good luck charm for Elvis—the Pelvis—Presley.

The 20-year-old rock 'n' roll singing sensation may not even be aware of it, but the reaction of an Indianapolis audience helped speed him on his bumpy road to fame and fortune.

True the sulky singer wasn't discovered here.

BUT IT WAS in Indianapolis that a "big time" agent first said "wow."

It happened this way.

Eight months ago Elvis was "one of the stars" in the Hank Snow troupe that began a four-day engagement at the Lyric Theater Dec. 4.

He was described as a "country and bop" singer and he was billed in type a few sizes smaller than that reserved for hillbilly star Hank Snow.

Local music critics ignored him.

And the hearts of only a few dedicated teenagers palpitated when they saw a picture of the sulky singer in The Indianapolis Times Dec. 3.

Mr. Presley was the "plus" in the show that starred Hank.

SNOW — the white flakey variety—detained Mr. Snow.

But according to observers, the Sunday audience became so intrigued by the gyrations and singing of Elvis, they didn't care that Snow failed to show.

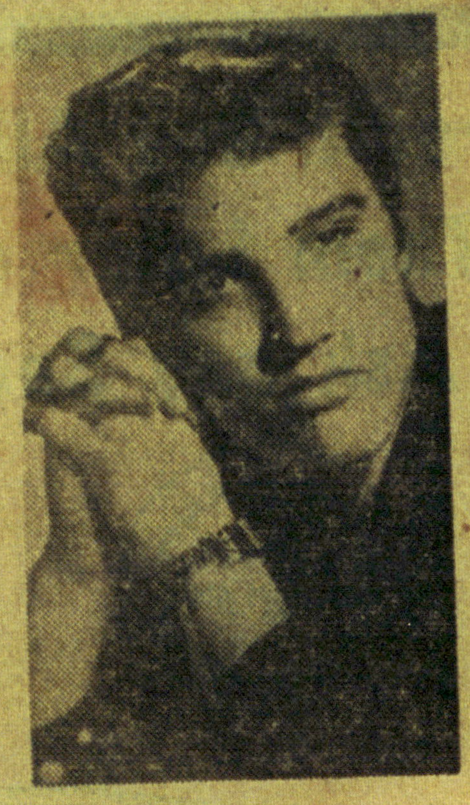

Mr. Presley

"They squealed every time he sang," recalls Dean Brown, then manager of the Lyric Theater. "When we saw him, we knew we had a hit."

Chicago agent Lou Mindling watching from the audience felt the same way.

"The record 'Blue Suede Shoes' was out. And my office, The William Morris Agency, was very interested," Mr. Mindling explained.

There had been some preliminary conversations with Col. Tom Parker, agent for The Pelvis.

"NEW YORK sent me to Indianapolis to look him over.

"It was a cold, snowy day I didn't think I'd find anything hot in Indianapolis," Mr. Mindling continued.

And then onto the stage stepped Elvis.

"I was very much impressed," recalls Mr. Mindling. So was the audience. It was tremendous. They sort of went wild."

Mr. Mindling told New York about the squeals and cheers, and the Memphis boy was later signed.

"With or without my recommendation or the Indianapolis reaction, it would have happened sooner or later," Mr. Mindling said. "He's wild and interesting."

Elvis visited the RCA plant while in Indianapolis.

The company had signed a recording contract with the singer just a few weeks before.

ange-
sley's
n and
were

om a
piece
Fan

who
FTD,
ent on
ral.
of the
emain
rs for
er Joe
ices.
as he
ades,"

not be
sley's
inger
ighted
al Ap-

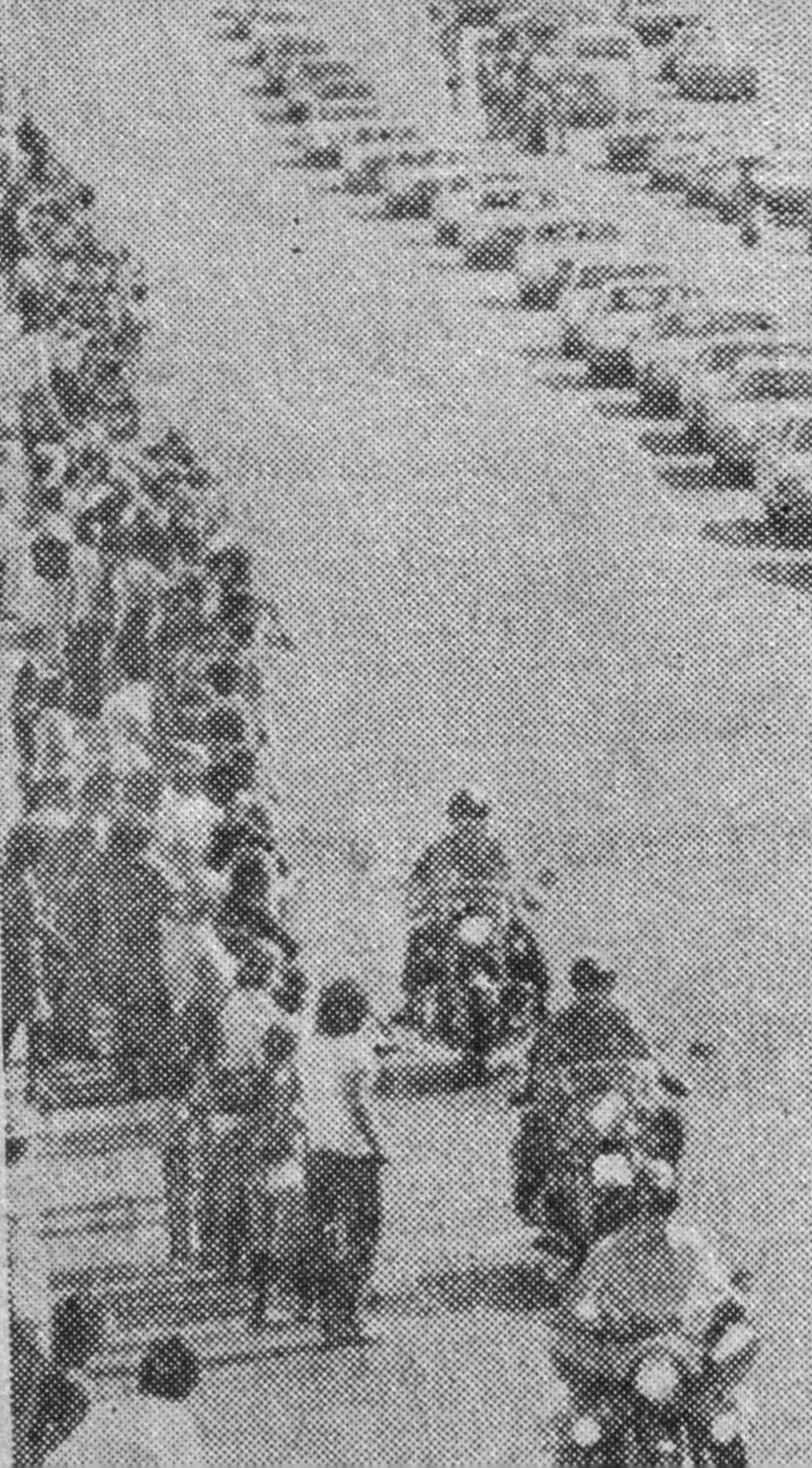